MINDFUL GRATITUDE

MINDFUL GRATITUDE

PRACTICING THE ART OF APPRECIATION

CHRISTEL B. WENDELBERGER

Published by Forward Communications

ISBN: 978-0-9992553-0-8

Cover Artwork: Timothy Meyerring

Book Design and Layout: Mary Phillips

Printed in the United States of America

For Michael, Luisa, Charlie, and George

With love and gratitude

Artwork, Journals Notecards, and More...

The cover of this book features, *Love Star*, an original painting by Timothy Meyerring, better known around the world as, Timo. His work is rich, spiritual, and easily communicates the language of the heart when words just won't do. Timo's work is used very intentionally in this book to touch that chord inside us all that responds intuitively to visual beauty.

Please visit our website, **www.mindfulgratitude.com** to order gorgeous Mindful Gratitude Journals, Notecards, and other products that feature Timo's practice of Mindful Gratitude.

Table of Contents

Introduction

This book was born a million times - with every sweet kindness, good lesson, misfortune, misstep, frustration, and glorious miracle that ever touched my life. My truest heart's desire is that it will be born a million times more in your life, with you as the author.

I believe that mystery, miracles, depth, and meaning are the essence of our existence. Mindful Gratitude is a simple but profound practice that allows us to access and experience these wonders at any moment we choose. Mindful Gratitude is the practice of looking up close at our sometimes messy, imperfect, busy, burdened, ordinary lives to see with fresh eyes the beauty, texture, depth, and color of our individual landscapes and the enormous contributions of humanity to our personal knowledge, progress, and well-being.

MINDFUL GRATITUDE

It is the practice of finding, noticing, and, most importantly, deeply appreciating the unique meaning and magic that are intrinsic in our everyday experiences.

These pages are an invitation to travel a little deeper into your life through Mindful Gratitude. They have been thoughtfully created and assembled with true love, deep respect, and genuine faith in you as an artist working in the medium of appreciation.

This book is not a set of recipes or prescriptions for a better life. Through ten personal essays – stories of meaning taken from my own life as a mother, daughter, wife, sister, friend, and working woman - and based on common human experiences like birth, death, losing, finding, celebrating, and saying goodbye – I offer my own practice of Mindful Gratitude. In writing these essays, I found an unexpected treasure trove of insight and new understanding about the nature of this mysterious life on earth, and I am very grateful for the opportunity to share them here with you.

But the real point of this book is to help you find and appreciate your own stories with prompts and guidance to help you reflect, notice, write, and share. With practice we can develop the skills and ability to find more peace, joy, love, and even magic in our life experiences.

Reflect

After each essay you will find a series of Reflection Points. These are questions or statements related to the essay and designed to open your heart, mind, and eyes to the miracles in your daily life. You can use them as starting points for reflecting on and writing about your own interactions and experiences.

Journal

Using the Reflection Points as prompts, start a Mindful Gratitude Journal and see what you might find. In the process of writing, a magical thing often happens. As we choose words and begin to describe our experiences, previously vague or unformed thoughts and ideas come into sharper focus. As we articulate them, we find and reveal new insights, fresh perspectives, and deeper meaning. This is true even when we just jot down a few sentences. Use a beautifully designed Mindful Gratitude Journal, or whatever notebook you have at hand, to begin excavating and expressing the goodness and depth that is waiting to be discovered and appreciated in your life.

Share and Connect

Express your gratitude and love to the people who touch your life. The memories, ideas, and words of thanks that we share with others carry much more significance than we usually recognize. Passing on your thoughts and insights will surely be appreciated, and you might inspire your loved ones to begin their own practice of Mindful Gratitude. Using the beautifully designed Mindful Gratitude Notecards, or whatever cards or paper you have available, send some words of thanks to the people in your life.

You could also start a Mindful Gratitude book club so that you can share and discuss your new insights. We also invite you to visit **www.mindfulgratitude.com** or follow us on social media. At the website you can order Mindful Gratitude Journals, Notecards, and other products and share your thoughts, experiences, and stories of gratitude to spread the love and expand the conversation about the natural beauty of our human experience.

With that, I humbly offer these personal essays, experiences, and ideas and invite you to turn the page, open your heart, and deepen your own awareness of all the wonder that surrounds us.

Bright Glimpses

One early spring morning I woke up and felt a tiny bird inside my heart. I lay perfectly still in my warm bed and somehow had the presence not to ask myself why a bird was in my heart. I kept my eyes closed and felt its soft flutter. Gentle. Innocent. New like a baby. I never felt anything like this before. Pure good. Pure happy. Coming from inside.

As my senses heightened, I tried not to think. I wanted to *feel* the love from this tiny creature. I felt her inside my heart and then on top of my chest. Her flutter wasn't anxious. Not like butterflies in the stomach when you first fall in love. But the bird did love me. She was joyful and warm and alive. And she opened the door to my heart.

Like in a dream, when one thing is two or three things, I also sensed the bird as a soft, white mist – breathing, yet formless. I smiled as the mist tickled my heart, and I realized quietly that *this* was my soul. This was my soul as a tender, loving, palpable reality – ready to be known. Again, I resisted the urge to analyze, to wonder, to move. I lay as still as I could and beamed with sheer joy at my enormous good fortune.

Eventually, I had to get up and live the life that I created here on earth. For a good while that morning, I could still feel the white, misty bird vibrating inside my heart. I held her there and thanked her for her visit for as long as I could. Soon enough, my brain was buried in my work. The phone was ringing. My list of daily tasks grew longer. And my mind took charge. Throughout the day I paused to see if I could still feel the bird's wings inside my heart. That day, I could.

As more days passed the tangible sensations of the bird faded. Her flutter became a sweet memory. But the lesson of her revelation remained. The bird was a whisper from my soul. She was my soul. She was me. Her visit was a reminder that life is a beautiful mystery and so are we.

Beneath the thick layers of projects, plans, responsibilities, errands, worries, thoughts, and emotions that dominate our days, there is something deeper and more real than we usually dare to be. There is a soul seeking to show us a peace and goodness that cannot be found in our world of challenges and mind-made solutions.

I wish I could say that I was dramatically transformed after the visit from the bird. That she led me to mastery of internal balance and harmony. But transformation is rarely dramatic. Most of the time it's a gradual process of incremental realizations and occasional bright glimpses of truth. In the quest for meaning, these bright glimpses are like celestial guideposts, indicating that we are on the right path and heartening us to travel on. My bird was a bright glimpse.

Bright glimpses shine into our lives all the time in all kinds of ways. Sometimes, they come in the form of a magical bird or a vivid dream. Sometimes, they sparkle through the innocent perceptions of a child we love or the world-worn insights of our favorite songwriter. They can come at church or at a rock concert. They are the telepathic phone calls from old friends on difficult days and the unexpected coincidences that remind us that our bonds with one another are deeper than we know. They are the experiences that transcend the ordinary and remind us to dream.

Bright glimpses give us some of our greatest opportunities to appreciate the human experience. And when we stop to recognize them, to really take them in, and embrace them with Mindful Gratitude, the magnitude of their brilliance grows and their ability to propel us forward expands exponentially.

Reflection Points

My experience and perception of the bird was a rare sort of bright glimpse into the peaceful joy that is at the center of every living being. Sometimes it can be difficult to notice these bright glimpses that shine into our lives. But most of us have experienced a time or two when our hearts felt unexpectedly full of love and connection to something greater than ourselves. The feeling, when it comes, can seem magical yet entirely REAL in the moment. Take out your **Mindful Gratitude Journal** and use the questions on the following page as gentle prompts that can guide you to your own bright glimpses of your personal truth. Or simply close your eyes and take a few moments to pull out a memory of a special bright glimpse. Acknowledge its lesson and shower it with gratitude.

> Have you ever been to a music concert and felt the power of connection that is created by the force of the artist and the shared appreciation for the music by the cheering, clapping, joyful crowd? Describe your memories.

◆ Have you ever been to a place of worship and heard a passage or an insight from a spiritual leader that opened your heart and mind to a new perspective?

◆ Have you ever had a vivid dream that brought you peace and comfort?

◆ Have you ever been thinking about an old friend when suddenly out of the blue, s/he calls to say hello?

◆ Have you ever had any experience that seemed out of the ordinary, unexplainable, and very mysterious? What truth did it lead you to? What mystery did it deepen?

Charlie Said

In the dark of his room, from the warmth of his bed and the depths of his heart, my son, Charlie, uttered the most profound little observation one night before falling into a deep sleep during the spring of his third-grade year. It was bedtime, and we were snuggled together on our sides. Nighttime prayers had been said. Philosophizing about the day was done. Charlie's eyes were closed, and I was thinking it was almost time for me to tiptoe out of the room.

Then, in a dreamy voice, Charlie said, "Sometimes, I am just amazed to be a person. Like, you get to walk around and do stuff. It's so cool. Life is like a game. Like in a game, you sometimes get in trouble and that's part of the game. And sometimes, I'm like—man, what are you doing? Just sitting around, being a hobo or something? Waiting to shrink down into a seed and be born?"

It was one of those rare moments when, as a curious questioning mother, I had the good sense not to probe any deeper. Instead, I let Charlie's reflection sink quietly into my heart as the tingle of his words danced up my spine. "That's beautiful Charlie," I said, touching his soft back. Charlie didn't say another word and was asleep in minutes.

I was left repeating his pronouncement in my mind. I found the closest pen and paper and wrote it out verbatim. Then I quietly basked in the light of a message that seemed to be channeled from a world beyond, yet entirely grounded in our earthly experience.

> *"Sometimes, I am just amazed to be a person.*
> *Like you get to walk around and do stuff.*
> *It's so cool."*

This is human appreciation at its purest. Gratitude for simply being alive, for the miraculous nature of every move, every thought, every experience that we get to have as human beings.

It's an expression of awesome wonder at the mysterious power that brought us to life and moves us through a world of color and form, light and darkness, music and wind, inventions and art that we can see and touch and hear and think about.

It's an intuitive awareness that indeed, we are, as Pierre Teilhard de Chardin, the French geologist, priest, philosopher and mystic said, "spiritual beings having a human experience." And it is amazing that we are alive in these most astonishing and intelligent bodies. From this perspective of innocent wonder, every moment is a gift.

> *"Life is like a game. Like in a game, you sometimes get in trouble and that's part of the game."*

This is wisdom at its deepest. No judgment. No resistance. No attachment. No pain. Life is like a game. We make decisions, develop relationships, choose our paths. Sometimes there are great triumphs. Other times there are missed shots and wrong moves. We make mistakes. And sometimes, for reasons beyond our control, things don't go our way.

> *"...you sometimes get in trouble and that's part of the game."*

Too often we misinterpret our "losses," placing heavy layers of judgment and blame over our mistakes. We spend time feeling sad or resentful about circumstances and outcomes that are out of our hands. We fight ourselves after the play is made, instead of simply moving on and accepting that sometimes, we're going to get into trouble. That's part of the game. It simply *is*.

From this perspective of acceptance, it's not our circumstances that matter. What matters is that there ARE circumstances, and the miracle lies in our ability to perceive them through our human senses.

> *"And sometimes, I'm like – man, what are you doing? Just sitting around, being a hobo or something? Waiting to shrink down into a seed and be born?"*

This is pure poetry. Vivid. Musical. Resonant. Soulful questions that came not from Charlie's thinking mind, but from a higher connection to something greater than himself. He evokes images of life's origin and its expanding and contracting nature, as well as the possibility that we are aware before we are born. Charlie seems to be asking himself and us not to take one moment of our lives on earth or one grain of our potential for granted.

On that cozy night in Charlie's room, it seemed like God himself whispered into our ears, reminding us to wonder. Reminding us to have fun. Reminding us of the open invitation to share in the adventure of life.

Reflection Points

Consider Charlie's thoughts about the nature of life and reflect on his lyrical, open-ended questions. Take out your **Mindful Gratitude Journal** and use some of the questions below to see what kind of poetry your soul creates. Jot down your responses to start creating a record of your own gratitude.

- What is the coolest thing about being a person? Is it the chance to taste delicious food? Listen to music? Create? Laugh with friends? Enjoy the beauty of nature? What are the things in this world that you love?

- What is the most beautiful or insightful thing that anyone has ever said to you? Who said it? What were the circumstances? What did it inspire you to do or feel?

▚ Remember a time when things did not go your way or you did not win one of life's games. What lessons did you learn? What positive impact did that situation have on your future? What are you grateful for because of that experience?

▚ "Man, what are you doing? Just sitting around, being a hobo or something? Waiting to shrink down into a seed and be born?" You ARE born. THIS is your life. What do you want to do, try, or experience while you are here? Make your list and have more fun!

Sunny Day Worm

I used to have a very bad habit. I would sometimes find it quite uncomfortable to wear my wedding rings. They felt binding and sort of aggravated my skin. Rather than bearing this slight discomfort, I used to take my rings off, no matter where I was, and carelessly stick them into my pockets.

I knew this was a bad idea, because one time, while wandering through a Sears store, I took off the ten-year diamond anniversary band that my husband Michael gave me, tucked it into a pocket that I knew was too shallow, and never saw the ring again. But bad habits die hard. So, for a long time, I kept taking my rings off and putting them into my pockets, half absentmindedly, half knowing I was flirting with danger.

Then one day I went to pull my rings from the pocket of the

pants I had been wearing the day before. My hand plunged into the pocket almost as thoughtlessly as it had when I stuck the rings there in the first place. I pulled out one ring – the golden wedding band that my mother gave us. I checked the other pocket and found a drugstore receipt for diapers and milk, a nickel, a Lego wheel, and my debit card – but not the second ring.

The diamond ring, the one Michael and I purchased together on a special trip, was gone. After a good search of the immediate area – the bedroom floor, the pockets of a few other pants that were lying on the chair – I thought, well, this has happened before. I'll just keep my eyes open. It'll turn up.

Days passed and the ring did not turn up. It wasn't in the kitchen or the bathroom or in my purse. I secretly wondered if maybe Michael found it and wanted to teach me a lesson by hiding it from me. I also feared the worst – that the ring went the way of the ten-year diamond anniversary band. That it fell out into the world, never to be seen by me again.

I tried not to obsess about the missing ring. With three kids, a husband, and my work, I really didn't have time to obsess about a missing ring. But worry simmered in the background, and I was more than a little disappointed with myself for neglecting a lesson I should have learned after the Sears incident.

Fortunately, that summer, I finally started a committed practice of mindfulness and meditation. After years of *reading* about the benefits of meditation, the power of NOW, the depth, richness, joy, and improved effectiveness that comes from experiencing the present moment, I made the decision to learn how to meditate and to make it a daily, morning ritual. I had the tremendous good fortune of meeting two wonderful teachers from India, the support of a dear friend who was also walking down this new path, and, *at last*, the necessary combination of desire and discipline to begin the practice of meditation and living in the present.

But what does it *mean* to live in the present? As a beginner (and I suspect I will *always* be a beginner) I take it to mean, at least in part, paying closer attention to everything around me – the sounds that I hear, the temperature of the air, the colors of the things I see, the textures of the things I touch. As a beginner, my attempts to be present don't always succeed.

My mind, like most typical human minds, is easily drawn into the melee of all that "needs to get done" – the calls to make, the e-mails to send, the projects, the shopping, the dinners, the bills, the kids and their whole lives. During any random three-minute period, my overactive mind might flit from thoughts of cleaning the bathroom to the state of global affairs to where my kids will go to college and *how exactly* we're going to pay for it, back to "Geez – I need to pick up some paper towels."

So one sunny morning a few weeks after the ring disappeared, surrounded by the hopeful atmosphere of my new commitment, I woke up and started my day like any other. I stretched. I meditated. I drank coffee and worked in my office for a couple hours. Then, when I heard a hint of stirring below, I headed downstairs to spend the rest of the morning with the kids.

It was warm and lovely outside and still quiet in the house. Only Charlie was awake, and he was ready to eat. Searching for a gallon of milk for cereal, I set out to the garage and the second fridge to see what I could find. As I walked on the sidewalk through my backyard, I had to step over a long earthworm who was stretched out over the cement.

It seemed odd to see a live worm relaxing on a sidewalk on such a dry, sunny morning, and I was briefly reminded of how much I loved worms when I was a kid. I loved to watch them, and pick them up, and wonder about them. The memory was so vivid, yet seemed so odd. Mostly, because as a city-loving adult, I cultivated an appalling, even embarrassing, *lack* of appreciation for nature.

As I got to the garage and punched in the code to the automatic opener, I thought about what a great invention the garage door opener is. Then I thought about ALL the button-punching inventions that we take for granted every day. Our lives are filled with gadgets and creations that make things move or cook or calculate by what seems to be pure magic, but which actually reflect humanity's amazing ability to harness the forces of nature for our collective growth and convenience.

Two hundred years ago if someone had suggested that humans would soon fly through the heavens in winged planes and rockets, or talk to each other on tiny, handheld wireless devices from anywhere around the globe, or look at images of the insides of our bodies and know with certainty the gender and condition of a baby months before she is born, it would have all sounded like pure, crazy magic. The speculators of such fancy might have been declared insane or blasphemous. Yet somehow, in a relatively short time, human beings have cracked essential codes of the physical universe to bring us all of this and so much more.

As the huge garage door opened at my button-punching

command, I started to think about some of the things that leaders at the vanguard of human potential are saying today that sound to lots of people like pure, crazy magic. Fantasy. Impossible. I thought about the medical pioneers who are teaching people how to heal themselves through meditation and visualization. I thought about the spiritual and intellectual leaders who believe that we can direct the enormous internal energy that exists inside the human mind and body to attract and achieve exactly what we want in life – the relationships, jobs, homes, experiences, everything.

I wondered whimsically if someday we might learn to direct human energy like laser beams to produce what we want with rapid speed. Will my grandchildren be able to blink their eyes like magical genies to produce lunch on demand? More seriously, will they know how to use the energy within them to guide their lives with deep precision, avoiding the meandering, unconscious choices and mistakes that create so much stress, anxiety, sadness, and destruction in our personal lives and the world?

With these lofty thoughts dissolving, I reached for the milk and tried to bring myself back to the present moment. I pressed those magic buttons to close the garage door and headed for the house, noticing the feel of the cold, heavy milk in my hand.

The long earthworm was in the same place on the sidewalk. But instead of stepping over him, I decided to do what I would have done as a child. I stopped to observe him and wonder about his world. Then, to make it more fun, I went to get my 8-year old son, Charlie, to watch the worm with me.

Charlie came out of the house, wearing a messy morning hairdo and his boxer shorts, to sit with his mom on the sidewalk and watch a worm. Quietly, we observed that the worm was so simple, sort of like one long muscle, yet moving using the same energy and source that animates our own complicated, thinking, interactive human bodies. And *moving* he was.

The worm started crawling at a rather quick speed. Squeezing and stretching his purple-gray body in a very specific direction. Without words, we continued to watch. The worm inched toward the edge of the sidewalk where the cement meets the grass. He slid down from the cement into the grassy ditch and took a hard left. Suddenly I saw something golden underneath some old dry leaves. Before I could even process what I saw, Charlie yelled, "Mom! Your ring! What is your ring doing out here?"

Stunned – really truly stunned – I picked the ring out of the grass, blew the black dirt from it, and stared at it in the palm of my hand. Was *this* an example of the magic of the universe

I had just been wondering about? Had my internal energy or intuition directed me to watch the worm so he could show me where my ring was? Why was a worm out on my sidewalk on such a dry, sunny morning anyway? Did he know me? Was he waiting for me? Waiting to say:

> *"Hey. You. Grown-up lady. Remember me? Remember how you used to focus on me like I was all that mattered, and hold me in your hands without fear, and think about the mysterious dirt and earth that is my home? Remember how you entered my world completely, laying your head on the warm grass, never worried about dirt or germs? Remember how you gently pulled the blades of grass from their roots so you could stare at them and imagine how they grew?*
>
> *WHERE HAVE YOU BEEN? Why don't you pay attention anymore? All the richness and wonder you loved just a few decades ago is still right here under your feet. If you're willing to pay attention, the world will show you everything."*

That day the worm showed me something that the great scientists, inventors, artists, and spiritual teachers have known forever: Presence is the gateway to the secrets of the universe. In paying attention, in noticing the smallest and seemingly most insignificant of things – like a thick earthworm relaxing on dry cement – there are grand discoveries to be made. In quiet, mindful observation we can find answers to our deepest questions – even those we didn't know we were asking.

Since that mysterious, miraculous, sunny day when the worm showed me my ring, I have cherished it as a sacred symbol of the essential importance of paying attention to my life and staying connected to the present moment. As a beginner I am far from living every moment in the present. My copies of various books by the world's great spiritual teachers are dog-eared from my constant need for reference and will forever have a place on the nightstand next to my bed. But I am absolutely committed to practicing a life of presence and gratitude – and so very grateful for the sunny day worm who shared his secret with me.

Reflection Points

Finding the ring was an amazing moment for me. If Charlie hadn't been there to see it too, I would still wonder if it really happened! And while the incident itself was certainly incredible, the real lesson of the experience is to stay alert to what life presents in any given moment. Cultivating the ability to observe life, with the curiosity of a great scientist or artist or unencumbered child, offers a brilliant key to discovery, truth, and enlightenment. Instead of simply walking on the earth, I am reminded to take time to walk *as part of* the earth, acknowledging the natural world on every level, including the tiny universe that lives beneath our feet. In your **Mindful Gratitude Journal**, consider writing about some of these questions and ideas:

Close your eyes and remember a quiet activity that you loved as a child. What was your favorite thing to do when you were alone - drawing, pretending, playing with worms, building with blocks or Legos, digging in the dirt? What details can you remember about those activities? Why did you love them? How did you feel when you were fully immersed in those moments of peace and focus and flow? Describe your memories.

◈ Observe the natural world. Find a living plant, tree, grass, insect or animal to observe in your home, yard, or neighborhood. You could even watch a person or persons, if you are able to watch without interacting. Observe for five or ten minutes, noticing the colors, rhythms, and movements of your subject. Describe what you see.

◈ Have you had an amazing or spiritual moment in your life when the normal rules of physics or logic seem to have been suspended? Describe the circumstances of the experience. What was going on just prior to the experience? Write down whatever you can remember. Who can you thank?

◈ What puts you into a state of flow or presence? What activities in your work, personal life, relationships, or free time require or bring about a state of presence? Describe the activities and how you feel when you are in the flow.

December's Natural Record

The Christmas card was beautiful as usual. Each year, my mom chooses a card that radiates her deep faith; something depicting mother and child in golden shimmer, or a classic nativity scene dominated by the light of the star that guided the wise men. She inscribed the type of message that I have grown to love, wishing my husband and children and me success and happiness and blessings at Christmas time and throughout the new year. But that year, after her loving wishes, she just signed Mom. Dad passed away in February, and this was our first Christmas without him. The card, signed only by Mom, was another tangible sign that it was official. Dad was gone from our midst.

For years I have been fascinated by the way that holiday

cards trace the prominent outlines of our lives, creating a natural record of a family's waxing and waning. It first struck me the year one of my uncles died. When I opened the Christmas card from my aunt that year, I stared at her singular signature for a long, long time. When I was a child, cards from Aunt Marilyn were filled with the names of my aunt, uncle and their five daughters. One by one, those daughters had grown and married and their names dropped off the cards. Then it was just my aunt and uncle. Now, just my aunt.

Initially my small anthropological discovery gave rise to a definite melancholy as I noticed the difficult changes and inevitable losses that come with being human. But the colorful envelopes that brighten our mailboxes during that last, darkest month of the year tell many stories. Mostly, they tell the story of life's enduring hope.

For just as surely as the names of my cousins disappeared from their parents' cards, they reemerged, inscribed upon new cards alongside the names of new husbands, like fresh branches on the Christmas card family tree. A few years later those pairs of names became three, four and five names printed under annual Christmas photos of adorable babies, toddlers and growing children. Thirty years later we are starting to receive a new generation of cards from those babies who have grown and started their own adult lives and marriages. What a privilege and a gift to share in the sprouting of each new branch.

No doubt, the messages and signatures on holiday cards tell their stories in scant detail, yet the themes remain powerful in their simplicity. Many years ago another of my cousins, a young woman in her twenties, passed away unexpectedly. That year, or maybe the next, her parents' Christmas card gained the name of her precious five-year old son, the grandson, for whom they would now be parents. Through the quiet inscription of signatures, that card tenderly held an untold story of loss, adaptation, resiliency, and family love. It reminded me that, despite experiences that can seem unbearable, human beings have an infinite capacity for moving on, living life, and taking care of one another.

The year my dear father died, my own family Christmas card marked another miraculous evolution. An unexpected pregnancy took our family by storm. Our two marvelous, dark-haired, hazel-eyed children, both of them long out of diapers and solidly into their school years, were joined by another brother. Now, to our amazement and joy, our annual Christmas card photo included a beautiful blue-eyed baby who looked every bit a genuine Christmas angel. As my mom signed her card alone that year, I took enormous pride and deep comfort in adding my dad's brand new namesake, a baby called George, after the names of his sister, Luisa, and brother, Charles, to our family card.

In the photo next to the message, the three of them, George in his sister's arms, stood smiling in the winter snow. They made it through a year that at once introduced them to morning sickness and ultrasounds, cancer and chemotherapy, birth and death. The greeting on the card simply wished our friends and family peace, love and prosperity in the new year and always. Our five names, listed after the greeting, an end-of-the year testament that our branch is strong and life is good.

Each December, as the holiday greetings start to fill our mailbox, I remind myself to savor their loving messages and untold stories. Mindful that our time on earth is finite, I find meaning in looking deeply at each name signed inside every special card; each one a sacred life on an individual journey.

I take time to look carefully at the photos of the children of friends whom I never get to see anymore and the ones of my nieces and nephews, most of whom I see all of the time, but whose beauty I often fail to take in completely during the typical rush of family gatherings. I read the long letters that some people take time to write, and I remind myself to acknowledge all of the unspoken courage, the quiet moments of doubt, the private tears, and the inevitable determination behind the news of family trips, graduations, weddings, passings, and new babies that often come with holiday greetings.

Imagining the cards as a colorful matrix of a lifetime of relationships, I relish the historic generational links represented in cards from our oldest relatives, the unbreakable bonds with old friends with whom we traveled or went to school in our youth, those who are now spread far and wide, but who continue to stay in touch at least this one time during the year, and I marvel at how new relationships continue to blossom as our children grow and connect us to a world of new friends.

This vast natural record of our lives truly confounds my imagination, leaving me humbled, enormously grateful, and reminded to thank my dear family and friends for taking the time to carry on the beautiful tradition of sending Christmas, New Year's, Hanukkah, and other holiday cards. Their messages, photos, signatures, and letters are deeply cherished symbols of our lasting connections and endless blessings.

Reflection Points

Envision the colorful matrix of your lifetime of relationships. In your **Mindful Gratitude Journal** write about just one of the changes, large or small, that you have noticed in your life or the lives of your friends and family in the past year. Birth, death, graduation, divorce, bankruptcy, new job, new house, etc. Find an example of life's undercurrent of hope and continuity within that change.

Think of all of the people who send you a holiday card at the end of the year. If you don't participate in a tradition of holiday cards, just think about the people in your life. Use the questions below to help you make a short list of some special people. As you write each name, pause in gratitude for their presence in your life. You might even want to jot down a line describing why you are grateful for each one.

- Who is your oldest relative alive and/or still sending a card and how far back can you trace the connection?

- Who sends a card from the most far away place? What friend or relative lives farthest from you?

- From whom have you been receiving cards the longest? Who is your oldest friend?

From whom did you receive a card for the first time ever this year? What new person came into your life in the past year?

Who in your life experienced the most significant change over last year?

Whatever time of year it is, use a **Mindful Gratitude Notecard** to send a special note of gratitude to someone you love.

February Winds

My father passed away during a dark and windy snowstorm on an early February morning. After hours of whispering the prayers of the rosary into his ear, my mother stepped out of the room to call their priest. I went in to sit next to the bed and hold Dad's hand, certain that after our month-long vigil, this had to be the end. Dad's eyes were open. He was conscious, but unable to speak. As I caressed his hand, a hand that had taken care of me for 41 years, I promised him I would stay until it was over. He nodded through his gasps and his body succumbed within minutes.

There is no way to deny the surreal pain of the hours that followed. The empty, cavernous feeling inside my own body; the tearful calls to family and friends; the normal human responses to the physical loss of one loved so dearly. But in the month before he died, my father, who long ago planted the lesson of gratitude in our hearts, became a living example of grace, acceptance, and faith, whose love far transcended the hurt of those initial raw emotions and will no doubt sustain me for a lifetime.

Throughout a cold and snowy January, as the signs of death grew starker in my parents' home – the wheelchair in the corner, the loud, rhythmic churning of the oxygen machine, the emaciated, bed-ridden body – an incandescent undercurrent of life glowed beneath the surface and shone from the places that we cannot see or hear, but can only feel with our hearts.

● ● ●

The illness itself was relatively brief. The diagnosis came late in the spring, with a six-months-to-live prognosis. The summer was filled with barbaric treatments. The fall was a roller coaster ride. Claims of a miraculous cure, followed by a somber pre-Christmas meeting at which the doctor said, in fact, the cancer had spread like dandelion seeds in the wind throughout Dad's body. It would be impossible to contain or to stop.

He could try another round of chemo, but ultimately, the result would be the same. Though he had been an extraordinarily youthful-looking and living 71, Dad's long, warm winters in Florida with Mom, his beloved wife, were over. No more golf.

No more poolside cocktails at five. He wasn't going to see any grandchildren graduate from high school, let alone college. He would not be at their weddings.

On January second, just two days into a year that he would barely know, Dad stopped eating. The feeding tube that kept him nourished for the past six months now delivered only pain. The doctors suggested he stop using it. There was really no decision about staying home to die. That was just the way it would be. My fiercely independent mother would care for Dad, with minimal help from the hospice people, who brought pain medication and officially checked his vitals every few days.

My husband, Michael, gave me the precious gifts of time and freedom at the end of Dad's illness, and I left our home to spend what turned out to be a full month staying with my parents. I took our five-month old nursing infant, while Michael stayed home with our two older children.

My three brothers and their wives were also visiting Dad daily. Four siblings, four spouses, ten grandchildren, along with neighbors, aunts, uncles, friends, and a couple of priests, were in and out of my parents' condo for weeks, bringing food, prayers and comfort. This was how my parents had always lived, with the doors to their home wide open. Still my mother managed to create a protective cocoon of privacy around our immediate family, allowing us precious days, hours, and moments with each other and with Dad.

● ● ●

The atmosphere in my parents' home that month was tender and profoundly honest, and until the final few days, Dad was fully engaged. There was no pretense or hiding from what was going on, and we did not restrain our emotions or our truths. We cried freely. We told Dad how much we loved him. We told him how much we would miss him – his advice, his support, his sense of humor. We thanked him repeatedly for his fatherly love and devotion.

We've always been an affectionate family, but while Dad was sick, we touched him more than we had since we were children. We kissed him and sat close to him. My brothers and my husband helped Mom lift him from wheelchair to bed. They shaved his sunken face. My brothers cradled him tenderly in their arms, holding him up when Mom brought the tiny shot glasses of crushed pain medication. We scratched his back and ran our fingers through his hair, which had returned from its chemo hiatus, dark and curly and soft. We noticed that without the thick glasses he wore our whole lives, how beautiful his eyes were – hazel brown, framed by long, black lashes.

Dad took it all in like an innocent child. He loved having us in the house those final weeks and unabashedly relished all the special love and attention. With such a captive and ever-present audience, his always quirky sense of humor was in high gear. Between our tears we were often hysterical with laughter as he told stories from his youth, or even made fun of his final situation.

One afternoon, early in our vigil, my husband stopped by to visit. "Michael!" Dad called, with as much enthusiasm as his weakening form allowed, "Grab a beer. We're all just sitting around on death watch."

When the phone rang, Dad would open his eyes wide and whisper, "Don't answer it. It might be God."

And he assured us that any troubles we might be having would soon be over, "Because," he would say, pointing to the sky, eyebrows raised, "as soon as I get up there, I'll start rearranging the scoreboard."

When his three grown sons worked together to lift Dad into his favorite chair or adjust him in his bed, he called them his "Three Musketeers," and gazed at them with the sort of childlike admiration usually seen on the faces of small boys looking at their fathers. Dad also fawned over my mother,

45

repeating things we heard him say all our lives, now with more sincerity than ever. "Your mom is the most beautiful woman in the world. Your mom is the best cook. Your mom always welcomed everyone into our home, and she always did it with class. No one is more caring than your mom."

Dad's focus was completely on us. His family. Under circumstances that were, by most interpretations, dark, Dad shined a light on the people he loved and made his last days somehow joyful.

● ● ●

The constant presence of our baby, George, named for Dad, provided another shimmering source of light over our vigil. For as we cared for Dad, moment by moment, at the end of his life; we also cared for the all-consuming needs of an infant. Georgie didn't know his Papa was sick. Changings, feedings, and his need to play and cuddle were not suspended like the rest of regular life had been that month.

The tasks and rituals of tending to my father's dying became warmly intertwined with the rhythm of tending to the needs of a new life. Mom and I took joy in giving Georgie baths, his soft, plump body and angel wisps of hair a striking contrast to Dad's gaunt skin and bones and a rich reminder of life's unrelenting renewal.

Nursing a baby, which I have always treasured as one of motherhood's most precious gifts, took on even deeper significance in the space of my father's vigil. Every few hours, when Georgie started to wriggle and fuss with hunger or thirst, my body's unconscious, instinctive ability to nourish his, reminded me that I was, above all else, a sentient expression of life's endless abundance. Warm, breathing, feeling proof to me that there is no loss, only transformation.

In the moments when sadness swelled, the presence of a baby buoyed our spirits. Grieving friends and relatives who stopped for short visits and left Dad's room in tears, softened to smiles when greeted by Georgie's bright eyes and baby squeals on the other side of the door. Happy to be passed around, Georgie became something of a human security blanket, accepting snuggles from all of us when we needed reassurance.

From his bed or chair, Dad cared for Georgie too. If he looked around and did not see or hear the baby, he would ask me, "Where's Georgie?" If Georgie got fussy, Dad would speculate about what might be bothering him. "Is he hungry? Does he need a change?" If I entered the bedroom without the baby, Dad asked, "Is Georgie okay? You didn't leave him alone on the couch, did you? He's not old enough for that." This was the type of banter I would miss so much when Dad was gone. "Dad," I would answer, exasperated, "Georgie is my third baby. I know that I can't leave him alone on the couch."

● ● ●

Through excruciating pain Dad never complained. He never once asked, "Why me, God?" And he did not spend time lamenting the things he would not see in the future. Yet there were moments when the realization that he had actually reached the end of his life clearly struck him. While he delighted in our presence, the surreal fact was that we were there saying goodbye to him – forever.

His happy childhood, his adventurous youth, his years of marriage and raising four children, all the decisions, work, relationships, struggles, good times and bad – were now behind him. All that he consciously knew of life was going to end, literally, any moment. He was going away, and none of us would be going with him. Despite his deep faith, he did not know what the moment of death would feel like or where exactly the angels would take him after that moment passed. "Nobody knows what it feels like to die," he said, "How does it happen?" But he approached even these questions with wonder and curiosity, not fear and anguish.

More than once Dad succinctly reminded himself, out loud,

of the series of events that led him unexpectedly to his death bed in the prime of his retirement. *"I got cancer,"* he would say, *"We tried to beat it. I took the treatments, but it didn't work. I'm going to die. And that's that."*

And that was that. There were no regrets. He simply accepted that this was how it played out for him. And he was profoundly grateful for the intense family togetherness and opportunity for conversation that this style of passing offered him.

● ● ●

Each night that month we gathered around Mom's and Dad's bed to tuck Dad in and to say his prayers with him. Though the hospice people offered a hospital bed, Dad refused, choosing to sleep with his wife in the bed they shared for 43 years until the end.

Some nights our bedtime crew was small, just one of my three brothers, Mom and me. Other nights, all my brothers were there. On a few occasions a grandchild or one of our spouses was still at the house for bedtime prayers. Most nights our baby George was there, in someone's arms, his blue eyes and fresh baby soul casting the glow of life's promise over the words of our prayers.

Together we said the three Hail Mary's that Dad prayed every night since he was a little boy. Then Dad just talked to God and to us. He said repeatedly and with genuine astonishment, "I am the luckiest man in the world to have this beautiful family here with me at the end of my life. God has blessed me with so much. It's truly unbelievable."

One night, with his hands folded and eyes closed, Dad prayed, "Lord, thank you for this wonderful day, filled with so many wonderful opportunities to learn new things."

●　　●　　●

On the surface the prayer seemed ludicrous. Dad was learning about the worst kind of physical pain and deprivation. He was learning what it felt like to starve to death. What it felt like to have your body engulfed in disease. But the "new things" to which he referred were not the things of this world or his physical body. These "new things" were surely the province of the heart and soul.

One afternoon, after he became totally bedridden, I was alone with Dad, sitting next to the bed, quietly holding his hand. As I sat there wishing I could take the suffering away from him, I remembered the story of Jesus praying in the garden of Gethsemane the night before the crucifixion. In the story Jesus prays in anguish, asking God his Father to let the cup of suffering pass over him, though accepting that God's will shall be done. He also asks his friends to BE with him. He asks them to watch while he prays. Yet they cannot stay awake and he finds them sleeping, unable to keep watch.

In that moment I understood an essential lesson of that story. It occurred to me that all I could do for my father was BE with him. There was nothing more. No one could take away his cup of suffering or reverse his fate. Our gift to him was our conscious, watchful, presence. As this realization settled into my awareness, I began to focus on giving Dad my full presence through our hands.

After a long while Dad broke our silence. "What are you thinking about?" he asked me. Surprised by his question, I didn't answer with the full context of my thoughts. Instead I said, "I don't know. Just thinking about how grateful I am to be here with you."

Then, Dad took in a long breath. "Oh," he said, with matter-of-fact presence, "Because I can feel a slight energy moving from your hand into mine."

This must have been the kind of new thing Dad was grateful for learning in that last month. Because, although he was always a spiritual man, talk of energy flowing from one hand to another, was simply *not* part of Dad's vernacular. But Dad had entered a state of grace. And in that state he transcended the confines of all that typically holds us back from fully feeling the multidimensional wonder of our universe, including the living energy that flows through each of us.

Through total surrender and complete acceptance, Dad shed the layers that typically block our perception of the magnificent and the mysterious. Physically, Dad disappeared before our very eyes, left without strength and nearly without form. Intellectually, he shed his ego. Politics and philosophies, postures and positions; the mind structures and beliefs that often leave us trapped in a flat and isolated personal existence, simply fell away. Dad was pared down to his essence - a repository of God's light. Clear, lucid, life energy.

Living in a state of presence, gratitude, and intuitive love, Dad developed a heightened awareness of the palpable stream of life – both the life we can see and touch in our physical world and the underlying life force that connects us to each other.

● ● ●

In the end, Dad's passing was a multi-layered lesson in living; a lesson too deep to sum up neatly in any essay. In many ways, it is all still a mystery to me. "Did that REALLY happen?" I sometimes ask myself. Is he REALLY gone? Where IS he? I think about that final month every day – sometimes in mourning, but mostly in awe of life's messy perfection. Because as blessed as we were to have our father raise us, we were, perhaps, equally blessed by the way he left us. In the prime of our parenting years, our careers, our marriages – the years of life fraught with striving and distraction, carpools and homework, decisions, doubts and sometimes, regret – Dad demonstrated for us, in the most dramatic fashion possible, what really matters.

In his final act of fatherhood, Dad showed us that it is our own ability to see the beauty inside of the people we love that has the power to transform us. When we look beyond ourselves, when we remove the veils of judgment and expectation to truly see and appreciate our family, friends, co-workers and even our "enemies" – we have the power to overcome any pain, any fear, any indignity, any humiliation, ANYTHING. Through unconditional love and gratitude, we have the power to connect with the source of all life, to transform our suffering into joy and death into life.

Dad passed into another realm on Ash Wednesday, the first day of Lent on the Christian calendar and a fitting day to say goodbye to this world. Ashes return to ashes. Dust returns to dust. But the inner light is everlasting.

Reflection Points

Dad was genuinely surprised by the outpouring of love and affection that rained down on him when he became ill. How did he not know that he, himself, had been the rainmaker through a lifetime of good living? I would venture to guess that Dad, like most of us, most of the time, didn't fully grasp the cumulative impact of his life's actions on the people and the world around him. He knew it was important to be honest and kind and generous. He knew that choosing goodness had better results than the opposite. But he just didn't know *precisely* how his choices touched his family and friends, until, when he became ill, the cards, and personal visits, and acts of kindness, converged and enveloped our entire family with a message of gratitude for my parents' lifetime of love and generosity. This reminds me that I need to tell people more often, on a regular day at home or work, exactly how their contribution to my life – on that day, or in general – is unique, and valued, and meaningful to me.

Use your **Mindful Gratitude Journal** to write about the best lesson anyone ever demonstrated for you. Describe how they brought the lesson to life and the concrete impact of their contribution on your life and learning.

▓ Write about a time when your connection to someone "transcended the confines of all that typically holds us back from fully feeling the multidimensional wonder of our universe." Have you ever been so connected to someone, whether alive in this world, or deceased, that your communication transcended the ordinary? Have you experienced telepathic communication or a tangible sense of another person's energy? Describe the specific situation and what it meant to you.

▓ Who in your life touches you deeply? How can you let them know now, while they are healthy and here in our realm? Use a **Mindful Gratitude Notecard** or any notecard or stationary that you have at hand to write a loving note to a parent or someone else who is dear to you. Tell them exactly what they mean to you. Be specific about the kind of contribution they have made in your life and how your life is different because of them. Thank them.

Sometimes the most profound moments of gratitude come when all is lost. Sometimes when it seems that you have nothing, it is easier to see that you have everything.

Fire & Grace

On an unusually balmy Friday evening in April of 1989, my family's spacious suburban home burned to the ground in a devastating fire. My parents were driving home from dinner at a local supper club when they first heard the sound of the fire engine sirens. Eventually they were behind the fire trucks and followed them all the way to their own front door where flames were eating my mother's dream house, a modern tri-level that she designed and built just six years earlier.

I was a senior in college and living in an apartment near campus, about 25 minutes east of my parents' home. On the night of the fire, I was out with friends - drinking, laughing, watching bands in a bar downtown – oblivious to the life-altering events taking place just a few miles away. It was an era before cell phones, texts, and constant communication. My parents didn't try to contact me that night, but if they had, it would have taken until two in the morning, when I finally rambled back to my apartment.

While I partied with friends, my parents and the oldest of my three younger brothers watched through the night as an unprepared and woefully under-qualified volunteer fire department failed to extinguish the horrifying blaze.

Unbelievably the suburb my family lived in did not have a professional fire department, and our neighborhood was completely lacking fire hydrants. Although dozens of volunteer fire fighters were on the scene within minutes of getting the call reporting a small garage fire, they arrived without a plan. Within twenty minutes they used up all of the water available on their trucks, NONE of which even hit the fire because their hoses were improperly aimed. Within six hours the fire obliterated what took my parents 25 years of married life to build.

The volunteers were unaware of a hydrant that could have been accessed through a field behind our house. They failed to call in professional support from nearby communities. And they never attempted to pump out thousands of gallons of water from the pool in the backyard. All of which my desperate parents suggested that night, and all of which were later determined to be reasonable options that might have made the difference between a partial and a total loss.

They also did not allow my family to attempt to save any belongings, although that too seemed to be a reasonable possibility. Since the fire started in a far corner of the attached garage, it actually had to burn that structure first, then break through a fire wall to get to the house. For a long hour before the house caught fire, my family, the volunteers, and a growing group of neighbors, stood and watched the garage burn.

When my brother asked the volunteers on the scene if he could enter the house, which was not yet on fire, and gather a few items – at least the special things, like photos, personal mementos, the keys to his classic car which was parked outside of the garage and which could have been put into neutral and pushed off the driveway to safety, the volunteers refused his request, and the gut-wrenching watching went on into the night. A slow, painful burn that lasted until the entire frame of the house fell into the basement.

A neighbor who witnessed the whole event caught much of

it on video tape. To this day I have not watched that tape. But we have been told that since it captures so many of the fire fighters' mistakes, it has been used in fire fighter training courses as a textbook example of what NOT to do when fighting a fire.

Very early on the morning after the fire, the phone rang at my apartment. It was my mom. She calmly explained that everyone was safe, but that our house burned down overnight and everything they owned was gone. Everything. She asked if there was someone who could drive me "home" to be with them.

I was bleary-eyed and confused. I remember saying, "Mom, it's early – is this a joke or something?" She said she was serious and repeated her question about someone being around to drive me home. My long-haired boyfriend (and yet-to-be-known future husband) was asleep on my couch, so I said, "Yes, Michael can drive me. We'll be there as soon as possible."

On the drive, I worried. I cried. I was shaky. What would the house look like? What does it mean to lose everything? Why was this happening?

When we rounded the corner onto our street and got our first glimpse of the scene, I gasped in shock. Then the tears began to fall faster. All that was standing was a portion of the front façade of the house. The rest of it was GONE and smoke was still smoldering up from the pit that was the basement. We parked on the street and I tried to suck in my tears. But at the first sight of my dad, who was standing on the front lawn surveying the damage, I fell apart like a toddler.

My parents had not been given anything. They earned every bit of their success. They made good decisions. They sacrificed in the old-fashioned way to build a life of financial security and creature comforts for their children. Now here was my dad, standing in front of a scorched pit of rubble with no more than the clothes he was wearing. From the eyes of a 22-year-old daughter, the snapshot was heartbreaking.

But in the split second between catching my dad's eye and hearing him speak, I knew that heartbreak would not be the overarching theme of this family chapter. Dad greeted us with a big genuine smile and a hug that I can still feel.

As I dropped into his arms, sobbing, he said, "Bing," calling me by the nickname he used far more than he ever used my real name, "don't cry. This is the luckiest day of my life! Everyone in this family is alive! The boys are safe. Mom is safe. Even that damn dog got out!"

And he was completely serious. Dad was HAPPY. He felt immense gratitude. "Look at what that fire did, Bing," he said, pointing to the wreckage. "Can you imagine what kind of day this would be if one of the boys had been in there?"

I barely began to digest the "tragedy" of my parents' loss when my dad proclaimed the day a "triumph." His perspective was not a surprise. Nor was it the shocked reaction of a man in denial. This was a case of values being tested and confirmed.

Forever my dad had been telling us, "Everything I have is on loan from God. None of this stuff is really mine." While tremendously grateful for any worldly or monetary success he achieved, my dad was not *attached* to any of it. It did not define him. It was not what counted.

Our home, our possessions, our comforts were things to enjoy and to share. They made life easier, and some of them were lots of fun. But in the end, they were only things. They did not have hearts to cherish or souls to nurture. They were fleeting, one-dimensional, and destructible. Now all of Dad's things were destroyed and all that was left was all that mattered to him – the people that he loved.

Shortly after we arrived at the scene, my mother came out of the next door neighbor's house to greet us. These neighbors were actually my mom's cousins, and after the fire was almost out, my family spent what was left of the night camped out in their living room.

At the sight of my mom, the tears bubbled again. We stood embracing on the front lawn for long minutes. My mom had dreamed of building the home that burned since she was a child. Maybe since her very first memory - of a fire that destroyed the house she lived in when she was just three years old. Maybe since her family spent two years living in a garage after her father returned home from the War.

From the comfort and security of my own childhood, I always found the stories of Mom's first fire, and subsequent life in a garage, impossible to comprehend. But I was certain about one thing. These mythical events from my mother's unimaginable past provided our family with a solid shield of protection. Who experiences two fires in a lifetime? Most people don't experience one. I figured my mom (and by association, the rest of us) was inoculated against fire by that long-ago tragedy that took place in the black-and-white world of the 1940s.

When Mom talked about that first fire, she always said that if we ever had a fire at our house, she would run straight to the family photos and save them above all else. That seemed like a good plan. But a plan seemed wholly unnecessary. I was POSITIVE another fire could not, would not visit her life.

But now I stood clinging to Mom in front of the ruins of her dream. As implausible as it seemed, a second fire came to incinerate all of her worldly possessions. I felt guilty and foolish for my immature confidence that such a thing could NEVER happen. And I felt inept and unqualified to offer words of comfort to the tenacious mother who had worked so hard to make life so much easier for her children.

Then Mom stood back to speak. "You have to come and see something." It was Mom's turn to confirm her values, her belief that all things are possible, that God does not abandon us, and that miracles do happen. "There was an absolute miracle last night."

Together we walked arm-in-arm into the kitchen next door. There, on the table, were eight of our family's most precious photo albums. They were charred and smoky, but completely intact.

"Our baby books survived," she said. "Isn't this unbelievable? These are the ONLY things that were not destroyed."

Before I could ask how *anything*, let alone fragile photo

albums, could have withstood a fire that annihilated a car, a garage, a house, and all of its contents, we sat down to look through the albums, marveling at each page as if it were a rare jewel.

When we were little Mom had four photo albums engraved with the individual names of each of her children. She filled each book with pictures that featured us in our most famous moments. Coming home from the hospital, first days of kindergarten, first communions, our best building block castles, birthdays with cousins, my brother Joe's mouth surgery, trips to the Grand Canyon, the beach, and our great great grandpa's cottages way up north – precious growing-up moments preserved in our four books.

Mom also took us faithfully to be photographed at a fancy studio downtown – every few months when we were babies, then every year until we went to elementary school. She had a full collection of classic portraits of all of us at every stage of development. For some reason she never hung these photos on the wall and instead chose to keep them inside of our four books. As a result all of them were spared from the fire.

My parents' thick white wedding album was on the table too, filled with photos that I spent hours staring at as a young child, enchanted by Mom's velvet dress, her draping bouquet of roses, the huge old city church, and the beautiful, happy faces of my youthful parents, aunts, and uncles. They looked like old time movie stars to me, living in another world entirely from the one in which I knew them as a child.

A couple of other albums were there too, including a golden clasped antique book of photo portraits taken in Montreal of mostly unknown ancestors, passed down from my Great Great Grandpa La Blanc.

Thousands of family photos and slides were destroyed in the fire, but our most precious pictures, the ones my mom hand-picked as her favorites, her *wedding album*, our *only* family heirloom, were miraculously plucked from the smoking wreckage undamaged.

It *was* unbelievable. How could these albums have survived? They had been stored in a built-in wooden cabinet in the lower-level family room. After the fire there was nothing left in that room. No furniture. No electronics. No toys or games. In the place where the piano stood, we found nothing but its wire strings lying in neat rows beneath the ashes. The fire burned so long and so hot that everything simply disintegrated. Disappeared. Everything except the cabinet that held the collection of family photo albums.

After the fire almost burned itself out, around two or three o'clock in the morning, one of the volunteers - a rookie, an eighteen-year old kid, who was the son of good family friends - jumped down into the hole that was the family room. Using a flashlight he moved around the debris to see what he could see. In the far corner of the room, next to the ruins of the fireplace, his light fell on the cabinet. He must have been astonished to discover the small sideboard, charred, but still standing, with all of its contents safe and sound. And I can only imagine how proud he felt crawling out of that gloomy pit with those eight precious photo albums in his arms.

This same young man went on to become a highly regarded Special Agent in our state's Department of Justice who was shot while working undercover as part of a high intensity drug trafficking operation. He was just 34 years old when he died a week later. It was his mother who bravely eulogized him in front of thousands of friends, family members, and fire and law enforcement officials. As part of her beautiful tribute, she recalled one of his earliest heroic actions; his caring bravery on the night of our family's fire.

My mom doesn't remember the exact moment he handed her the books. But one of my cousins who was there said that Mom clung to the books, saying, "My babies. My babies. This is unbelievable." My cousin also told me that they spent a long while paging through the albums and walking down memory lane during that first dark night.

The books offered solace in the immediate, unthinkable hours just after the high-drama of the fire was over. Just about the time my parents and brother must have been exhausted. Just about the time they must have been saying, "Let's brush our teeth and go to bed." Just before they realized - in a split-second of confusing clarity - that they no longer had beds. Or toothbrushes. Or pajamas. Or any of the other hundreds of tiny personal comforts we take for granted every day.

They woke up the morning of the fire in a beautiful, sturdy home surrounded by the physical illusion of security. By bedtime it all had vanished - all but eight priceless photo albums that were somehow touched by the light of grace.

In the days and weeks after the fire, my parents moved on, taking care of business like always. They rented an apartment and began making plans to rebuild.

Meanwhile their friends, family, neighbors, and even strangers, gathered around them in a warm circle of support. Just hours after dawn, on that first day after the fire, the flow of love and generosity began to pour into our lives. People started showing up at my cousins' house with gifts, hugs, and food. Casseroles, cookies, sandwiches, and snacks. Sustenance and distraction on a day that was impossible to fathom.

A week or so later, friends and family hosted a huge "shower" for my parents - a luncheon and gift opening in the style of a traditional wedding shower. People brought beautiful wrapped presents: dishes, sheets, a coffee maker, toaster, baking pans, and household gadgets of all kinds.

The final gift presented to my mom and dad was an address book that had been completely filled out with the names, addresses and phone numbers of everyone at the party. My parents were reminded that all of these people were just a phone call away if they needed anything at all.

When lunch was served, our family went through the buffet line first. As my dad sat with his lunch in front of him, he watched his friends, brothers, sisters, and neighbors walk through the line – talking and laughing like they would at any family gathering. Overwhelmed by their goodness and generosity, Dad wiped tears of love and gratitude from his cheeks - the only tears I saw him shed after the fire.

Now that I am a grown woman, with a family and home of my own, the magnitude of what happened to my parents is much clearer to me. I simply cannot imagine the trauma of helplessly watching my home burn to the ground. And I cannot imagine dealing with the massive upheaval of losing everything. I'm pretty sure the odds are on my side that I won't have to – but I never say *never* anymore.

Life is unpredictable. Our possessions are temporal. A fire, storm, accident or umpteen thousand other random events could upend our carefully built, planned, and plotted lives at any moment. How *would* I react to a major disaster? I don't know for sure. But as I reflect on my parents' response to their fire, I wonder if it is more important to ask myself how I react to the mini-disasters that are far more common in our daily lives.

When I get stuck in traffic and I am late for a meeting. When my four-year old throws a temper tantrum at the breakfast table. When a client is difficult. When my husband and I just can't agree. When an unexpected expense obliterates my monthly budget. Do the values that served my parents so well guide and save me from my own manufactured frustration, anger, sadness and despair?

Can I see the grace that surrounds me on any day, under any circumstance, and find the authentic sense of celebration and gratitude that allowed my dad to stand in front of his burned down home and declare with all sincerity, "This is the luckiest day of my life!"?

What is my relationship to my possessions? My things may bring me physical and psychological comfort, but genuine security comes from within.

Is my heart open to miracles – like fragile books withstanding the heat of a devastating fire? The more our eyes are open to life's possibilities, the more likely we can see the miracles that constantly touch our lives.

Do I look for the goodness and generosity that lives inside of everyone? From the friend who invites our family for dinner, to the stranger who holds the door for me at the store, contentment comes in recognizing and honoring the sacred acts of kindness that we experience every day.

I can see now that it was a clear value system that represented something bigger than themselves that pulled my parents through such an extraordinary situation. Gratitude, grace, and generosity - indestructible truths capable of withstanding the force of an earthquake, the power of a tornado, the heat of any fire, and the intensity of our darkest fears.

Reflection Points

Thankfully most of us will never experience the total loss of a house fire, tornado, war, or other natural or manmade disaster. Still we all experience what might be considered loss, personal tragedies, disappointments, or challenges. There are the big and dramatic events like a car accident, serious illness, job loss, or the death of a loved-one that seems to have come far too soon. And there are the much more common and mundane challenges like dealing with a difficult co-worker, missing a flight, or misplacing the car keys. Elements beyond our control have the power to rearrange our carefully laid "plans" at any moment. This is the nature of life. Changes will come that we have not chosen. But the gift of human awareness, consciousness, or free will, DOES provide us with personal control over our response to these unexpected, and sometimes unwelcome, changes. And our responses in the most difficult moments are primed by the values we hold dear and the mental, emotional, and spiritual beliefs that we practice on a daily basis.

In your **Mindful Gratitude Journal**, take some time to reflect on the values and beliefs that you hold dear.

Can you see the grace that surrounds you on any day, under any circumstance? List some examples.

What matters most to you? What do you believe in that is bigger than you? How do these beliefs and values help to carry you through some of life's difficult situations – large or small?

Can you remember a time in your life when grace, gratitude, or generosity saved you from your darkest fears and most difficult challenges?

Can you recall a kindness (small or large) from a friend, family member or stranger, that particularly touched your heart and shed a little light on a dark day? Use a **Mindful Gratitude Notecard** or whatever paper or stationary you have handy to send that person a thank you note.

What is your relationship to your possessions?

Is your heart open to miracles?

Do you look for the goodness and generosity that lives inside of everyone? List some examples

Profits of the Heart

For memory has painted this perfect day with
colors that never fade.

These simple, evocative lyrics, written in 1910 by the legendary American songwriter, Carrie Jacobs-Bond, are fittingly etched around the small silver frame of a treasured photo taken one perfect summer day. It's a close shot of my daughter Lulu, her beloved cousin Calvin, and Lulu's oldest friend Eva – best friends and the firstborn children of three grown college roommates.

The kids are three years old, and the girls are wearing matching sleeveless cotton dresses in yellow and lavender. Calvin is in the center with the soft, tanned arms of the girls wrapped around him so insistently that one little hand is holding his face. The girls are smiling serenely. Calvin's smile is bigger, more mischievous, and his eyes are cast playfully off to the side. The August sun glows so brightly behind them that, in my imagination, its rays have formed halos around each of their precious heads, reaching beyond space and time, shining perpetually.

The photo sparkles from a shelf in Lulu's teenaged room – an ever-present reminder of the goodness of summer, friendship, and life. To me it's also a reminder of the indelible imprint of love that can be left on our hearts forever by the passion, creativity and hard work of certain visionary individuals. It was taken at Gil Fest, a local street festival that ran annually for ten magic-tinged summers when the kids were all young.

Gil, a dear family friend and the singular creative force behind Gil Fest, owned Gil's Cafe, a unique, two-story, corner restaurant just a couple of blocks from our house. Cherished by neighbors and a steady troupe of regulars, the restaurant was open seven days a week, offering delicious brunches, lunches, dinners, strong coffee, and a full bar.

Gil's was one of those rare spots where everyone felt comfortable. An exposed brick interior and idiosyncratic artwork mingled casually with wooden schoolroom tables and chairs, old-fashioned lace curtains, and flower vases on every table to create an ambiance that was hip and homey all at the same time.

Gil was a professionally trained chef who graduated from the Culinary Institute of America. He opened the restaurant when he was in his early thirties. A quiet, handsome man with a thick crop of dark hair, Gil presided over the cafe with a gentle friendliness and quirky sense of humor. Never a flamboyant show-off sort of restauranteur, his presence was nonetheless constantly felt as he often emerged from the kitchen in his white chef's coat to quietly visit with guests or joke with servers who gathered at the bar.

The cafe's menu reflected Gil's culinary expertise, but Gil's other passion, maybe his deeper passion, was music – rocked-up, bluesy, countrified Americana music - to put a finer point on it. The kind of music that banks on soulful rhythms, pared down strings, and rich harmonies. The kind of music that cries and laughs and celebrates the human experience with an independent, nonchalant swagger that is distinctly American. Gil was a tremendously knowledgeable aficionado with an academic grasp of the history and trajectory of the genre he loved, and a heartfelt affection and respect for the craft of songwriting, the magic of live performance, and the eclectic artists themselves.

Shortly after opening the Cafe, Gil started hosting small acoustic shows in the upper level dining room. While working seven days a week, cooking and running the restaurant, Gil was quietly cultivating relationships with his favorite local and national performers and their managers. He started drawing artists from Austin, Nashville, and other points south up to our cold Midwestern city to a venue that could hold 100 fans tops. Eventually, performers like The Silos, Chris Stamey, and Joy Lynn White, along with old-timers Sonny Burgess and Billy Lee Riley, Sun Studio recording artists who got their start with Elvis, and young up-and-comers like Carrie Rodriguez, made stops at tiny Gil's Cafe a part of their national tours.

For artists touring the country in vans and playing mostly big impersonal bars and clubs, Gil's must have seemed like an oasis. Gil treated the musicians like special guests in his home. He cooked for them, stocked their favorite drinks, and made sure they were comfortable in every way.

Audiences embraced the shows and were grateful to Gil for the gift of such unusually intimate live performances by artists whose tours probably would have skipped our city, had Gil not personally invited them to play here. Gil was brokering relationships between artists and audiences, connecting the music he loved to the community he served and creating a touring demand for a genre that had long been absent from our local music scene.

At some point Gil had the idea to host a one-day Tex-Mex style summer music festival on the quiet, tree-lined street just outside the restaurant, and Gil Fest was born. My husband Michael and I attended the first Gil Fest with Lulu when she was just a year old. That first year the festival was small. We ate tamales and drank cold beers on picnic tables in the street and kept our baby out late, cozied up in a stroller with her favorite blanket. There was a small stage set up under a white tent, lit by soft pink and yellow toned lights. The crowd was modest too. We sat with Gil's family all night - his wife Mary and her sister Margaret, their brothers, and their parents — some of our favorite, funniest friends in the entire world.

That first understated Gil Fest lives in my memory like a sweet dream. We talked, we laughed, we ate and drank, and we were blown away by the bands and performers we heard that night. The afterglow lasted for days. I bragged endlessly to friends and family who missed the inaugural Gil Fest, explaining that we had to hope Gil would do it again next year and warning that they absolutely could not miss it if he did.

Gil did do it again the next year - and for another eight years after that. Each year the festival grew, the stage got bigger, the entertainment started earlier in the day, and the memories made grew grander and more magical. The crowds grew too. Gil Fest turned into something of a late-August reunion for friends and families from near and far. Our brothers, their families, my parents, a few cousins, and assorted others from our family tree attended several Gil Fests, as did the parents and families of other friends.

And the circle of friends seemed to grow each year. Old pals from college days, Michael's band days, neighbors, colleagues, new friends and their friends. For a full decade they all made Gil Fest a regular destination on their summer social calendars, giving Gil Fest the feel of a multi-generational game of one-or-two-degrees-of-separation.

At every turn, all day long, you ran into someone you hadn't seen all year, someone from the kids' school, an old friend with her new husband and baby or her parents who were in town for the weekend. It was one hug and smile after the next - a dot-to-dot maze of hundreds and hundreds of happy faces all connected to each other in one way or another.

Among our close-knit circle Gil Fest became a relied upon bright spot in the year. No matter what else might be going on in someone's life – we had Gil Fest to remember and Gil

Fest to look forward to. If we hadn't seen some friend all summer long we would say, "Oh well, we'll see them at Gil Fest." When someone needed cheering up, we might decide to rehash some happy moment from a previous Gil Fest.

Gil's love of the music, the artists, and their eclectic style infected all of us. We considered in advance what we might wear to Gil Fest, with some of us urban Midwesterners even buying cowboy hats, boots, or bejeweled and embroidered shirts, all in honor of Gil Fest's extravagant one-day tribute to the freewheeling, music-loving, American spirit.

As our families grew Gil added all kinds of fantastic activities for the kids. There were magic shows, games, face painting, pony rides and a petting zoo. Even the church across the street got into the act – giving out free hotdogs, snow cones, and water bottles during the daylight hours of Gil Fest. The kids looked forward to Gil Fest as much as we did. A day of slurping on endless snow cones and playing in the street with friends and cousins was surely the stuff of classroom daydreams.

Char-grilled burgers, tamales, and special attractions aside, Gil Fest was always about the music. Gil made major financial investments to book the best artists he could possibly attract, given the size and budget of the festival. He paid to have a

huge stage and sound system set up on the street, and
musical performances went from "High Noon to Midnight"
as the iconic promotional posters announced around town
all summer long. The daytime line-ups included mostly local
bands. But as the sun moved west across the sky, the acts got
bigger, louder, and more famous.

Around about the fourth Gil Fest, my husband Michael, who
spent his teens and twenties singing and playing in rock
bands, along with some other musician friends, formed a
band called Pinto that became known for their annual
appearance as the opening act at Gil Fest. They were a
group of thirty-something former rockers paying tribute to
the old-school country songs of the Louvin Brothers, George
Jones, Tammy Wynette and a host of other country legends
and the California country-rock sound of Gram Parsons and
the Flying Burrito Brothers, lesser-known, but critically
acclaimed predecessors of the music scene that produced
the Eagles and Jackson Brown.

For our kids it was a thrill to see their dad on stage, singing.
For me, it was a thrill to hear Michael's irresistibly sexy voice
radiating from the sound system, reminding me of how I fell
in love with him in the first place. I won't ever forget sitting
on the curb of Hackett Avenue, holding one of our children
on my lap, listening to Michael sing those old-fashioned

songs of heartbreak and betrayal. We could have just had a huge argument over any mundane marriage wedge-issue – laundry, dishes, who left the gas tank empty - but as soon as the first note fell from his mouth, I melted like butter in the late August sun and all else was forgotten.

For those of us with children, Gil Fest was split into two parts. Kids stayed and played from noon until a little while before sundown. Then a couple of the moms would walk a crowd of them back to our house where we would hire a sitter to care for the crew of cousins and friends while we went back to hear the main acts.

With the kids tucked away safely at home, nighttime at Gil Fest was a flat-out riot for the adults. Pure, rowdy, happy fun. The intoxicating combination of old friends, warm summer air, live music, and a variety of free-flowing beverages, made us feel like we were 21. The responsibilities of marriage, careers, and parenting were briefly released in waves of reminiscent laughter, tear-inducing harmonies, loud guitars and, now legendary performances by artists like Drivin' and Cryin', the Bottlerockets, and Alejandro Escovedo.

Gil Fest went on rain or shine. More than once, it rained, but Gil Fest was never rained out. One year a day of on and off drizzling turned into an all-out downpour just before the main acts were about to get started. Gil made the call to move the bands inside the restaurant, rather than cancel, even though the outdoor crowd far exceeded the capacity of the indoor venue.

As many water-drenched fans as could fit packed into the second-floor dining room to hear a raucous performance by the Jack Ingram Band. The crowd was bouncing and dancing so wildly that the floorboards of the century-old building were bending beneath our feet. We worried fleetingly that we might crash through the floor onto the diners below, but mostly, we laughed at our own antics until our cheeks hurt.

These were the simple values of Gil Fest: Have fun. Get wet. Love the music. Love your friends and family. Be happy.

But for all the carefree good times that happened in the space of the twelve-hour festival, it took a super-human year-long effort to actually plan and pull off Gil Fest. For Gil it was months of choosing and booking the best possible performers, seeking sponsors, ordering supplies, staffing-up, and living with the questions and queasy feeling in his stomach that anyone who has ever planned a big party can understand: Will it rain? Will people come? Will I have enough burgers and tamales? Will I have too much? As an entrepreneur Gil had one more high-stakes question:

Am I going to lose my ass on this deal?

Gil Fest put Gil way out on a financial limb. There were good years and bad years. Times when cash was stolen or the rain kept too many festival goers away for him to make up his investments. While we were dancing, socializing, and falling in love, Gil was sweating behind the grills, directing the action in the kitchen, hauling out beer and other supplies, checking cash drawers, and, when he was lucky, sneaking out to catch the performances of the artists he loved so much.

I always tried to find Gil at some point during the festival to thank him for throwing such a spectacular party for all of us. He always seemed happy - excited to be sharing the music and artists that were so close to his heart with whoever wound up on the street outside his restaurant that day. Sharing what he loved, after all, was the point of the whole thing. But it was also the risk. In creating Gil Fest, Gil laid his heart bare. Like any artist or entrepreneur, Gil put a piece of himself on display, giving life to his big ideas and transforming his personal passions into something that other people could hear and taste and experience for themselves.

It was a brave risk that ultimately did not pay out sustainable financial dividends. The final Gil Fest was held in August of 2005. After twelve years in business, Gil closed the restaurant under enormous personal and financial duress the following summer.

As is often the case when a business doesn't make it, there was nothing tangible left of the enterprise for the owner and his family to fall back on. No profits or savings to show for the years of long hours and personal sacrifice. No plaque for service and dedication to the community. The business closed, and Gil and his family were left with debt, disappointment, and a long grieving process, not unlike the kind experienced after the death of a loved one.

Many times during the difficult years that followed the closing of the restaurant, I wanted to tell Gil and Mary that all the hard work mattered more than money could ever measure. That Gil had, in fact, left an enormous legacy and created an infinite fortune too big to be calculated on an accountant's balance sheet. But in the face of a family's struggle to hang on to their home and take care of their kids, my existential musings seemed a little impractical, maybe even insensitive.

But the deeper truth is that Gil's Cafe and its infamous annual Gil Fest will generate profits of the heart for decades beyond Gil's lifetime - at least for as long as his children and his friends' children are alive and positively influenced by their sweetest childhood memories.

There is an ephemeral quality that is the essence of a festival, a show, a party, or any special place and time in life that belies a deeper sort of permanence. You can't hold events and moments in your hands or see them with your eyes after they have passed. You can only experience them while you are in them. The decorations, tables, stages, guests, performers and settings seem to just disappear, and the memories seem like a dream.

But like every strand of life that touches us, these memories are seamlessly integrated into the story of who we are. Whether we are conscious of them or not, they are there shaping us, influencing us, inspiring us even when we don't know it. Gil's imagination, hard work, dedication, and simple love of music created many lifetimes worth of grand and vivid memories and infinite waves of positive vibrations whose final destinations he will never know.

Sometimes in the middle of the cold dark winter, when I've got piles of work in front of me and no fun in sight, and going outside means putting on ten layers of clothes and big awkward boots just to push through heavy snow and whipping wind, I take myself to Gil Fest. I go to a specific moment in time when, for an hour or so, every single thing in the world seemed perfect.

Alejandro Escovedo, the 70s-punk rocker turned soulful singer/songwriter, was the headliner that year. During his performance, Michael and I stood next to each other and very close to the stage. The air was soft and warm late into the night, and the shadows of the wide green August leaves flickered and waved beneath the streetlights. My friends were nearby. My babies were snug in their beds down the street.

Alejandro performed a breathtaking version of his great love song, Rosalie, followed by an incredible cover of Mott the Hoople's All the Young Dudes. I breathed in all the details of that moment and let every drop of summer goodness sink deep into my heart.

On dark days, that memory inspires me and reminds me that life is good and the world is big. There is music, and laughter, and warmth, and love somewhere in every moment.

These are the lasting, massive, unquantifiable profits of Gil Fest.

Thank you, Gil. Thank you so very kindly.

Reflection Points

Most of us have a special restaurant, pub, store, gallery or some other place that has touched us positively or been part of a beautiful memory. These places exist because of the vision and passion of one or more individuals who wanted to share what they love with the world.

Review the Reflection Points below and remind yourself of something you love, send a card, write in your journal, or take a quiet moment to practice Mindful Gratitude.

Do you have a favorite restaurant, festival, place, or event? Who is responsible for its creation? How has his/her/their hard work, imagination, and willingness to share their personal passions positively impacted your life – for an hour, a day, or beyond? Use a **Mindful Gratitude Notecard** and send a message to the person/s responsible. Let them know how their vision has touched your life. If you don't know who is responsible for your favorite place, take time to write about it in your **Mindful Gratitude Journal**. Remind yourself of the details. Why do you love this place or event? How does it make your life richer or happier?

89

▓ Do you have a special memory of a place or event from your childhood, youth, or adulthood that has influenced, inspired or comforted you? Can you recall the details and jot them down in your **Mindful Gratitude Journal**?

▓ Next time you are in your favorite place, whether that place is a business or the home of a friend or family member, notice the details. Notice the flowers on the table or the choice of color and lighting. Someone made those choices based on what they love and because they wanted to make themselves and you more comfortable. Let it all sink into your heart for safekeeping until a day when you need a little inspiration or a reminder that you are loved.

▓ What is your passion? What do you love and how do you share it with the world or with the special people in your life? If you are not already doing so, can you find a way to share what you love? Make, bake, or cook a homemade gift; create and share a playlist of your favorite songs; or invite a friend to do something you enjoy. Jot down a few paragraphs about your passion and ways that you can share it in your **Mindful Gratitude Journal**.

Angels of the Border

Elias arrived in a catatonic state. The police brought him to us, because it was the only thing they could think to do. His thick, gray hair was wild, and an overgrown mustache and whiskers dominated his long, gaunt face. He came in a rickety wheelchair, wrapped in a dark wool blanket. Besides the clothes he was wearing, he had nothing. A tattered, stinking, abandoned Einstein picked up on the dirty, dangerous streets of Juarez.

It was dark when they dropped him off, and the guests were in bed. He needed a bath and a place to sleep. He also needed medical attention. His feet and legs were covered in red and yellow oozing sores. None of us were medical professionals, and it was going to take someone with a stomach of steel to care for his wounds.

This was the sort of situation that frightened me and led to serious self-doubt about my worthiness as a volunteer, maybe even as a human being. Cooking and serving rice and beans to seventy-five hungry men, women, and children was one thing. Providing medical care for a foul-smelling elderly man was quite another. We stood in a semi-circle around his wheelchair, quietly contemplating what to do next. To my relief two male volunteers, Jerry and Peter, stepped up and offered to provide the bathing and other personal services that Elias needed. With that the late-night decision was made to take him in.

A couple of months earlier, I arrived in El Paso on a cloudless Sunday afternoon. I was 24 years old, a year out of college, and still lacking any serious career experience or aim. I was tanned and relaxed from a summer of waiting tables, hanging out at the beach, and nightly parties. Though I remember virtually nothing about my departure from home that day, I remember in vivid living color the freedom of breathing in the big blue Texas sky when my plane touched down some 1600 miles and a whole new life later.

The El Paso airport was small and sparse, and I was picked up by a boyish young man named Noah. After awkwardly introducing ourselves he led me out to his beat-up, cream-colored station wagon. I tossed my bags into the back, and we drove away from the airport and into the biggest adventure of my life so far. I didn't know a soul in all of Texas, let alone anyone on the other side of the bridge that separated El Paso from Juarez, Mexico. I only knew that it was right for me to be there.

After the self-indulgence of my college years, I was compelled to go somewhere far away and do something well outside of my comfort zone. I had been a political science and peace studies student and a devoted news junkie, which, in the late 1980s, meant heavy daily doses of CNN and weekly cover-to-cover readings of *Time* and *Newsweek*. I read books like the *Tao of Pooh* and the *Autobiography of Malcom X* and took classes on race relations and religions of the world. I cared about people and issues beyond my little sphere, but from a very safe, very intellectual distance.

Like a lot of idealistic young Americans, I balanced (maybe even pacified) authentic sadness over the world's injustice with overindulgence in distractions like parties, concerts, and media. Now I was going to stop hiding. Stop pacifying. I was going to SEE life, FEEL life, LIVE life before I went out and spent the rest of mine working in some adult career that I still couldn't quite fathom.

I was searching for meaning in a world that seemed to my

young eyes to be fractured beyond repair by endless war, political injustice, and massive poverty. As idealistic and maybe even naive as it sounds, I wanted to understand firsthand the widespread economic and political suffering that existed beyond the confines of my privileged, middle class American life, and I wanted to be part of an organized effort to alleviate some of that pain. In a word, I was searching for compassion – my own and the world's.

My search was further fueled by the recent loss of our family home and all of our belongings in a ruinous fire. The day after the fire, as I stood in disbelief, staring at the smoke coming up from the pile of rubble, it was clearer to me than ever that our material world is fleeting and impermanent. It is what we DO, not what we HAVE, that has lasting value. It was time for me to wake up and do something.

Months after the fire I applied to be a full-time, live-in volunteer at one of two shelters operated by the same organization located on either side of the U.S.-Mexico border. My qualifications were light at best, but my application essay somehow convinced them that I had something to contribute to the organization.

Left out of the essay were most references to how I actually spent my time in that year after I finished school: Working in a quirky, family-owned Italian supper club with mob ties and a cast of characters worthy of a Scorsese film, hanging out with my rock musician boyfriend and his band mates, hosting parties at my apartment, and drinking in bars. We laughed a lot. We took it easy. We reveled in being on the outside of mainstream culture. I knew that life couldn't go on forever, but it was an awfully fun place to linger until I figured out what I was supposed to be doing with my life. Leaving for Mexico finally seemed like the thing I should do.

Though I was assigned to live and work at the house in Juarez, there was a week of volunteer orientation based at the house in El Paso. So from the airport, we went to the El Paso house and were immediately greeted by dozens of beautiful, smiling, Central American faces. The "house" was a repurposed triangular commercial building circa 1900 that had been transformed into a homeless shelter designed to accommodate about 75 people.

The "guests" were the poorest of the border's poor; at that time, mostly refugees from the ideological wars of Nicaragua, Guatemala, and Honduras. They were innocent men, women, and children caught in the middle of political conflicts from which they had little to gain and everything to lose. They were brave souls fleeing economic devastation and the kind of unspeakable violence and repression that I read about in

Time and *Newsweek*. Now, here they were in front of me, smiling, welcoming me as a fellow traveler who was far from home. The children gathered around with hugs. I doubted immediately that I deserved this loving reception. But I took it, tears streaming, feeling a bit like a thief.

Their journeys to this house in a rundown barrio had been arduous – hiding from guerrilla warriors and violent soldiers, sneaking over treacherous mountains in the middle of the night, risking life and limb hopping trains, and wearing down their feet with miles and miles of walking. The lives they left behind, while unimaginably difficult, still included families and home places and home sounds and home smells that would probably never be seen or heard or smelled again.

By contrast my "journey" was a pleasant direct flight that included lunch and cocktails, and the life I left was one of ease and frivolity. These penniless refugees were living on the very edge of life, in a strange country with no safety net, no possessions, and no place to return to. I had a credit card in my sturdy Jansport backpack and could have hopped back on a plane the next day if the volunteer thing didn't work out. This was a theme that would return to me day after day during my time at the houses. *How is it that I was born with so many resources and they were born with so few, and how could I live with a clear conscience on the weighted side of this random inequality?* At 24 my answers to these questions were often clouded by harsh self-judgement and a sense of guilt for a privilege I didn't ask for, but was nonetheless relieved to have. Twenty-five years later the answers are gentler and wiser, yet nowhere near clear.

The other volunteers also greeted me warmly. Someone gave me a tour of the house, pointing out the kitchen and the other volunteers who were making our dinner. That night it was rice and beans with tortillas and a little lettuce and tomato salad. They told me that, well, basically, every night, it was rice and beans with tortillas and a little lettuce and tomato salad. I didn't really like beans at the time, and this concerned me. But within a week, I LOVED beans and barely noticed the monotony of our diet. Mealtime, I quickly learned, was a time of joy and connection, whatever was served. Besides, every week or two, someone donated some chicken or avocados. Then one of the guests would show us how to whip up a delicious mole sauce or the best guacamole I ever tasted. Here, simple things were celebrations.

The houses were opened in the 1970s by a group of young people who sought simply to serve the poor. The organization grew somewhat organically and eventually found its work to be sheltering, feeding, and advocating for the poor and homeless of the border. To this day the houses function with an all-volunteer staff who consciously choose to live among the poor, with the stated mission of "mindfully transforming their understanding of what constitutes more just relationships between peoples, countries, and economies."

I was attracted to the organization because of the emphasis on volunteers living in solidarity with the people they were serving without hierarchy. We were to live at the shelter, prepare the meals, eat with the guests, and be conduits of caring. While we were there to be stewards of donated resources and do the actual day-to-day work of operating a house that held up to 75 people at once, our deeper purpose was to be truly present with the guests, to listen, to seek understanding, to bear witness to their struggle, and to help where we could. It was a simple, but profound assignment.

To help us mindfully process our experience in a more meaningful spiritual or social context, volunteers participated in a daily morning reflection, meditation, and discussion time. Here we cried about some of the things we had seen and laughed about others. We talked at length about the inequities we saw and asked ourselves deep questions about the balance between being present to suffering and taking action to end it. We asked ourselves where the personal ends and the political begins. And we returned again and again to the question of HOW we would return to our comfortable middle class homes knowing what we now know. Our serious questions were constantly informed by the profound lessons we were learning from the guests about presence, resilience, faith, gratitude, acceptance, persistence, and the power of loving kindness.

Most of the volunteers were also in their twenties, recently out of college or grad school, and searching for understanding. A few of them were in their thirties or forties and there were even a couple of Catholic nuns in their sixties. They came from all over the United States and beyond. All of them made a six to twelve month commitment to service, so there was a natural rotation of volunteers into and out of the houses. I was in awe of these smart, thoughtful, generous individuals and honestly felt rather unworthy of their kind, interesting, and unconditionally supportive companionship. Collectively they were some of the most remarkable people with whom I have ever worked. They were out to change the world, but they were not dour "activist" types. They were sweet and funny and vibrant. They shined and I was thrilled to stand in their light.

They were mostly from the United States, but we had a few international volunteers, including a young man from Pakistan who was from an enormously wealthy family that placed great expectations upon him after he completed his formal education in the U.S. He was to marry the woman of their choosing, pursue a career of their choosing, and establish himself at the top rung of Pakistani society. But this unusually kind and gentle young man developed an incredible sense of social justice and was terribly conflicted about returning to a life of extreme privilege in his country, where so many people lived in poverty. His search for a way to understand his own privilege and live a fair and just life balanced against the expectations of his parents in a society that formally stratified people by class and income was fascinating, and I felt so honored and grateful that he chose to share his search with me and the other volunteers.

After the initial orientation I was taken over the bridge to the house in Juarez, where I would begin my official service. Unlike the house in El Paso, where most of the guests were wading through the immigration and political asylum process and were unable to work legally, in Juarez, all the guests worked, and the house was closed between 8 a.m. and 4 p.m. During those hours all guests, except for those who were sick or who had small children, left the premises for very conventional factory jobs – the kind of jobs that fueled the massive growth of the middle class in the U.S. throughout the middle of the 20th century and allowed American workers to buy their own homes, and go on vacations, and send kids to college.

Juarez had become a hotspot for U.S. companies to build
factories where they could employ Mexicans at much lower
wages than U.S. workers – pennies-on-the-dollar lower. The
city was being flooded by immigrants from the impoverished
interior of Mexico looking for work. They arrived in Juarez with
nothing but a small bag and a burning desire to find work in
one of the shiny new factories or "maquiladoras" of the
border.

And it was as easy to get a job as they expected. The factories
were so big and proliferating so quickly that those who
arrived in Juarez on a Sunday could easily be employed by
the end of the day Monday. The problem was that they
arrived with no money and nowhere to stay, triggering a
homeless crisis that was exploding. Our little shelter was a
miniscule band-aid that covered only 75 people out of the
tens of thousands in need. Each afternoon when we
reopened the doors, we found a line of people that included
those who were allowed to come back from the night before
(typically, guests stayed for a few weeks before saving
enough money to rent a room or build a cardboard "house"
in the mountains of Juarez) and dozens of new arrivals hoping
to avoid sleeping on the streets with a safe bed at the shelter.

The volunteer in charge of opening the house first called out
the names of those who had been lucky enough to secure a

bed on the previous night. Any remaining beds were handed out to those at the front of the line. Then a small crowd of those for whom there was no room at the inn, would say "gracias" and shuffle back out into the streets. People almost always left quietly and very gratefully. It was a heartbreaking daily ritual.

Those who were returning from a previous night's stay usually came in and immediately offered to help with something. Most of them had just worked a long day in the factory, but entered the house with smiles and goodwill. I had never known people with so little. Literally they had only what they carried in, usually whatever they were wearing and a small bag with a change of clothes. The bags were often paper or plastic, and donated backpacks from our clothing bank were hot items.

In most cases they were earning anywhere from 80 cents to just over one dollar per hour, working jobs that paid $15 - $30 an hour in the U.S. I remember seeing one young man's first paycheck. He was 18 or 19 years old and had he earned the equivalent of $27 for about a week and a half of work. This was less than I made in a few hours of waitressing. Yet, he was proud and excited to have a start to his savings for a small rented room of his own. Never mind that the room would not have a private bath or kitchen. This young man was grateful for the opportunity to work.

About 75% of the guests were in their teens or twenties, traveling alone, looking to work. Another 25% were small families looking for the same. And then there were a few outliers. Elias, the broken Einstein who arrived at our door late at night, was an outlier. We guessed he was at least 65 years old and it seemed extremely unlikely that he would ever work again.

In fact, after being delivered to our doorstep, he sat silent in his wheelchair for nearly a month. We had no idea where he came from, what he did before he arrived, or whether he had a family anywhere. Day after day Jerry and Peter steadfastly cleaned his wounds, fed him, bathed him, shaved him, TALKED to him, and demonstrated the kind of compassion that inspired everyone else to talk to Elias, too, no matter how silent and mysterious he seemed.

Then one day, out of the blue, Elias spoke. He repeated some phrases that sounded like nonsense to us. But his vocal chords worked, he was forming real words, and he was making eye contact. The tenderness and loving kindness that surrounded him brought him back to life. A few weeks later he began to walk. It was a slow, shuffling, old man's walk, but it was a walk. He started to shower and shave on his own, and he became a helper to the volunteers. He sorted stones out of the huge buckets of beans that we used each week, set the long tables with forks and cups at mealtime, smiled and hugged and connected with the people that surrounded him. He even started dancing.

Oddly, living in a house with 75 rotating virtual strangers from all points in Mexico, the U.S., and beyond, gave Elias the opportunity to dance quite regularly. Impromptu evening dances in the dining room were a normal occurrence at the house. Someone would bust out a guitar or blast the latest Mexican radio hits on an old-fashioned boom box, and all the guests and volunteers would gather to dance and sing along and celebrate.

What were we celebrating? We didn't need a special occasion, though a birthday or holiday gave good reason to pull out all the stops. Maybe we were celebrating safe passage, or a good meal, or the fact that we all had beds that night – no one in this group of travelers ever really said. It was just the most natural thing to put on some music and dance.

Sometimes the celebrations were watered with teardrops. A wave of homesickness or weariness might overcome a guest or volunteer as he or she sang along to a classic Mexican ballad of the heart. When this happened the strangers of the house gathered around that person, literally offering shoulders to cry on and support to stay standing. A constant sense of community existed in the house, despite the transient nature of its inhabitants. We were all travelers just passing through – far from home and those we loved – dancing under a roof held up by a collective vision of love and generosity.

In addition to Elias the house had another long-term guest who often inspired the nighttime dances. Isidrio also arrived at the house in a wheelchair, but fully of his own volition. Years earlier, he lost his legs while attempting to hop a train. He desperately wanted prosthetic legs and the chance to walk again, but his family was very poor, and there was no way he or they could afford the legs.

Still, Isidrio was a regular viewer of an odd kind of television "game show" that was taped in Juarez. Real people went on the program to tell true sad stories and to beg for money or help from the public. Isidrio wanted to be on this program so much, that he took weeks to literally wheel himself hundreds of miles from his small hometown to Ciudad Juarez and the doors of our shelter. He was sure that if he could get to Jaurez, he could get a spot on the show, tell his story, and get the money for his legs.

Isidrio was a husky guy with a booming voice, and he loved

to sing Mexican ranchera music. He stayed at the shelter during the day and helped with all kinds of things, but I remember him best sitting in his wheelchair in our little kitchen, drying dishes, and singing at the top of his beautiful lungs about all matters of love and the corazon. He smiled nearly always, except sometimes when he sang and giant tears streamed down his cheeks. He missed his family terribly but was not planning to leave Juarez until he got on that program and could return home on new legs.

Isidrio was at the house for at least four months before I left, and made no progress toward getting on the show. Although I never said it to anyone, it seemed like a hopeless endeavor to me. But Isidrio never gave up hope. He believed in his unlikely dream without wavering. His faith was born out sometime after I left the shelter. I got word that he DID, in fact, get a spot on the show. Another of the volunteers sent me a photo of him on his prosthetic legs. He stayed in Juarez long enough to get the rehabilitation and therapy he needed to return to his hometown a walking man.

Through our daily reflections, we volunteers remained acutely aware of the difference between our experience and that of the guests. While we were all travelers, we had families waiting for us in homes that were literal palaces in contrast to the stark rooms and cardboard shanty towns to which our guests were headed after they left the shelter. We had degrees and could return to the U.S. to launch good careers with decent salaries. Most of the guests would toil in factories and might never live in a house with running water and electricity. Our questions about justice and our personal responsibility persisted, and so did my oversized personal sense of guilt.

Then, a week or so before I left the shelter, I came face to face with my internal guilt and turmoil through another unique relationship. A barefoot 14-year old girl had turned up at our door, wearing only a skirt and blouse. She had no bag and no shoes. She had no family and no friends. She was truly alone in the world. Fortunately, we had room for her that day and she was welcomed as a guest. I found her some shoes and a change of clothes in our clothing bank, and she was extremely thankful.

I was often baffled by the inequities I saw in Juarez, but this girl sank especially deep into my heart. How could she be so courageous? I could barely make my own dinner at 14, and here she was, out in the world, without shoes, fending for herself. I was in awe of her.

Each day I spoke with this sweet girl and we established an easy bond. One day, she asked if I had any photos of my friends and family to show her. In those days, before smart phones, people carried real photographs when they traveled far away. So I went up to my room and brought down some cherished photos from home. One was a professional shot from my brother-in-law's wedding, taken just before I left for Juarez. We were wearing typical American wedding garb, fancy dresses and tuxedos, and we were standing on the altar of a lovely church. She stared at my photos and then said, somewhat breathlessly, *"Ustedes son ricos."* "You're all rich."

I was embarrassed. Why did I share these photos that exposed so plainly the truth of my American existence? I felt insensitive and stupid. In six months, my polite Mexican friends never pointed out the disparities that we volunteers pondered daily. Now this young girl was calling it. She could see that I was from a world with everything, and she was from a world that left her cold and alone on the streets of Juarez. Would she be angry at the inequity? Would she think of me as a fraud? Would she reject me as a spoiled American princess?

As it turned out, she was much kinder and gentler with me than I had yet learned to be with myself. A few days later, when I was preparing to leave the shelter to go back to my home, she rushed to me in a panic before I departed. She said I could not leave because she had something for me. She ran upstairs and then back down to me, holding a wispy necklace. She wove it with two thin pieces of yarn and it had a cross at the center. She was weeping and thanking me for everything I did for her and wishing me safe travels. She said it was so important to her that she give me a farewell gift. I put it on and hugged her and told her I would never forget her kindness.

For a long time I felt guilty about this incident. I didn't deserve a gift from that child. I should have emptied my suitcase and left all that I had with her. Her beautiful gesture added to my general sense of mind-based anxiety about returning home to a life of comfort, having seen up close the kind of desperate poverty that plagues so much of the world.

It took years of growth and finding my place in life to let go of that guilt and finally acknowledge intellectually what my heart knew the moment I was presented with that black and white yarn necklace. It was a gift given without judgment of either one of us or our individual life or economic circumstances. It was given in the true and simple spirit of unconditional friendship, generosity, and gratitude.

Like Elias and Peter and Jerry who showed me the life-giving power of tender loving kindness, and Isidrio who showed me the miracle of tenaciously believing in one's own vision, and the countless other brave hearts that I encountered during my time on the border, this sweet child will always be an angel in my life, reminding me to graciously and joyfully accept the gifts I am given without judgment or guilt. More importantly the little yarn necklace reminds me to be generous with my resources, time, and material wealth. If a girl without even a pair of shoes could find a gift for me, I can surely find something to share with the world every day of my life.

Obviously I returned home and did not reject my life of American luxury – a sturdy house with running water, electricity and appliances, plentiful food, a car, clothing, healthcare – all of it. Instead I came to a slow truce with my guilt and chose to live in the place and circumstances of my birth with a higher consciousness about the responsibilities that go along with my privileges. My time in Juarez led to a long career in the nonprofit world; developing programs, writing grants, and telling the stories of people and organizations who are working to improve the world.

As a person fortunate enough to have been born into the Western World's middle class, I choose to live, not with a useless sense of guilt, but with mindful gratitude for all that I have and an awareness of how the lifestyle and economic choices I make impact people in my family, my community, and across the globe.

It is still a wonder to me that the predominant energy in those houses full of the poor and war-torn was always that of generosity and gratitude. The guests were not naïve. They understood, far better than any of us could ever imagine, the pain and hardship of war and poverty and separation. But they also understood how to live in the present and appreciate the good things that were close at hand.

They reveled in the deliciousness of a meal, the sweetness of a baby in the shelter, the thrill of finding a job, the connections that could be made with strangers sharing difficult circumstances, the sheer fun of playing music, singing, and dancing. They understood that when the good things in life present themselves, we need to celebrate them to the fullest, despite, or maybe because of, whatever darker circumstances may seem to surround us.

These courageous, hardworking, grateful people are still reminding me, through their extraordinary example, to SEE what I have in my life, to share it, and to celebrate it – no matter how big or small. My heart is filled with eternal gratitude for the angels of the border who showed me that there is beauty to be found in life – always and everywhere.

Reflection Points

⬥ Who has shown you the greatest loving kindness in your life? What did she/he/they do for you? How were you changed physically, emotionally, or spiritually as a result of this kindness? Describe these things in your *Mindful Gratitude Journal*, OR use a *Mindful Gratitude Notecard* to send your "angel" a message describing how their kindness touched you.

⬥ What is the most generous gift that anyone ever gave you? How did it change you? Describe it in your *Mindful Gratitude Journal*, OR use a *Mindful Gratitude Notecard* to send that person a message thanking them and describing how her/his generosity touched you.

⬥ Have you ever had a personal goal that seemed a little crazy on the surface, but that you achieved because you believed in it? Write about it in your *Mindful Gratitude Journal*. Be thankful to yourself for not giving up and to anyone else who helped to make it possible.

◆ Do you volunteer in your community? Write some notes in your **Mindful Gratitude Journal** about the great things you get BACK from volunteering.

◆ Use your **Mindful Gratitude Journal** to make a list of ways you want to be more generous with your time, talent, or resources. Then…TAKE ACTION!

Milano

Life felt far away the summer I met Milano. I was working too much, laughing too little, and living almost entirely in my head – hooked on problem-solving and strategies, immersed in work deadlines, and drowning in low-grade anxiety. By late June I had barely looked up from my internal, self-created pile of work and worry long enough to feel the season's glorious light and heat. A beautiful summer was going on just outside the smudged filters of my brain. If I squinted and pressed my face up to the glass, I could see it, but I just couldn't touch it. In a word, I was disconnected.

The work on my hands was not a figment of my imagination. For 16 years I had been operating my own full-time fund development consulting practice, mostly creating communications strategies and writing grant proposals to connect philanthropic individuals and foundations with non-profit institutions doing some of the most important work in our city. I served world-class arts organizations, museums, libraries, universities, schools, social service agencies, and major health care institutions.

These great organizations, their visionary leaders, and the philanthropists whose gifts bring services, performances, and ideas to life have been a source of deep inspiration to me. But my heart has always been most closely tied to the organizations that address poverty, education, and the creation of opportunities for young people living in our central city. Over the years I developed a special niche serving these agencies and telling their stories.

This work keeps me in close contact with the social and economic statistics that characterize the typical woes of a large American city and describe the cycle of poverty that is both cause and effect of broken families, struggling schools, crumbling neighborhoods, teen pregnancy, crime, violence, and human misery. My grant proposals outline the challenges and detail the solutions that organizations have developed to intervene in the lives of kids who need a pathway out of poverty.

The solutions are many, but the ones that work best weave

together an absolute belief in the potential of the human spirit with practical support and methods for teaching kids real-life skills that lead to success. These programs hold the conviction that every child has unique gifts and talents that need to be nurtured. Every child needs to understand how to set and achieve goals of their own determination. Every child needs positive activities and caring adult support. With these ingredients and access to the basics – food, shelter, education and healthcare – every child has the potential to succeed and achieve in school and life.

The opportunity to work on projects that reflect my deepest values is an enormous blessing. But, as with any kind of work, sometimes the end-goal can become blurred in an avalanche of minutiae, planning, personalities, and pressure. Raising money properly is a big-picture strategy game that also requires unfailing attention to detail.

In the non-profit world, especially at the level of small social service or educational agency, there is often just a tiny team of one or two professionals working to raise the entire budget of the agency. People's jobs and service to thousands of children often depend upon the fundraiser's ability to identify, attract, and maintain the right mix of donors. This is not a job to be taken lightly. Many of my clients are just these sorts of small agencies.

They consider hiring me an investment that MUST have a return. I take this responsibility very seriously, as I should. But occasionally, I wander mindlessly over the line of reason and lose myself in an imagined bottomless pit of too many deadlines, decisions, and details. During these times my perception of the whole world can turn dark, and I begin to feel like I live in an intellectual tunnel on a speeding train that only stops long enough to hit a deadline before taking off to hit the next one.

This, I suspect, is what happens to most of us. We take our work and our responsibilities in life so seriously that we begin to confuse those responsibilities with who we are. We become responsibility machines - thinking on high-speed, living weeks or months into the future, and completely forgetting to feel the earth that we walk on, the sun that shines on our skin, the soothing rhythm of our breath, the powerful beating of our hearts, and the invisible energy that connects us to each other.

Being connected emotionally to the issues and people that I am writing about is critical, but the act of writing is a solitary effort. And when the goal of one's writing is less to tell a straightforward story, and more to strategically move the reader to take a very specific action, like making a major philanthropic contribution, the people and circumstances written about can sometimes turn into intellectual abstractions blinking on a computer screen - sections to be covered, sentences to be tailored, well-chosen words tactically placed to stir passion and imagination.

From a small home office in a leafy urban enclave of historic homes, upscale shops, and views of Lake Michigan, I spend a good deal of time staring at a screen, writing about the needs and strengths of young people who live, *just over the bridge – on the other side of the river*, in neighborhoods dotted with boarded up homes and messy corner liquor stores. I write about their talents and aspirations and their right to the educational and social opportunities that could help them transcend crushing generational poverty and transform the segregated landscape of our city. I write about how their future is OUR future, how we are all connected, how our city can only thrive when all our neighborhoods are filled with hope and opportunity.

Meanwhile, during the busiest months of the year, my brain can become so preoccupied with these stories brewing in my head, that I am barely capable of genuinely connecting and interacting with the people in my own home, let alone those living in neighborhoods a couple of miles away. Instead, I can feel isolated, overwhelmed by the magnitude of our world's inequities, and trapped by the treadmill of deadlines, responsibilities, and attention to nit-picking details often required in the field of fundraising. Even worse, I feel like I have no time to pursue my own truest aspirations – my dreams of leaving the fundraising world behind and writing stories and poems and books and making art that is free of any strategic agenda. These dreams get buried, and I feel like I am stuck.

Such was my mood for most of that disconnected summer, especially on the day when Milano knocked on my front door. That day I was on deadline with a grant proposal for a client whose mission is to provide job training and entry-level employment to very low-income young adults who have dropped out of school or been in trouble with the law. The program is inspirational really, but that day, as I struggled to meet the deadline, I was just too distracted, anxious, and overwhelmed to connect with the material.

My work worries were compounded by a surreal and viscerally disturbing occurrence that was actively plaguing our home. For days our living room had been swarmed by slow-moving, pitch-black flies. Apparently, a small mouse had met its end within the chimney chase of our century-old home without our ever noticing. The evidence came with the flies that seemed to be very creepily crawling, not flying, out of the fireplace at a rate of hundreds per hour.

At first they trickled out a few at a time and we could simply wipe them up. Then they started coming so fast that if we left the room for an hour or so we would return to find hundreds of them crawling on the floor, the windows, the curtains, and carpet. Using the long hose attachment, we would vacuum them up, turn for a moment, and, as if by dark magic, more would appear in the places we had just cleaned. It was something directly out of one of my stress dreams and an eerie mirror of my own internal perception of my work and life that summer, triggering some of my most irrational and primal fears about life's illusion of control.

That day an exterminator was to come and make a recommendation. Though I should have been glued to my desk until the draft of my grant proposal was finished, my inability to focus led me to wander downstairs mid-afternoon to see what was going on with the rest of the family. That's when I heard my husband, Michael, talking with someone at the front door. Certain that it was the exterminator, I headed toward their voices to find out the plan for dealing with the unnerving infestation. But as I got to the door, I could see that Michael was talking with a young man, and the buoyant tone of his voice suggested sales, not extermination. In fact, it was Milano, standing on my porch to sell us magazines and break through the dense, dark fog of my present worldview.

When I stepped up to the door, Michael introduced us and immediately disappeared, leaving me alone to decide whether to close the door on this guy or not. Milano was wearing a slightly large, slightly dull, white button down shirt, black kakis, and a large salesman's smile. He was African American and looked to be in his early twenties. I said hello and thought about my computer screen blinking on the third floor and the client waiting for the proposal.

I don't have time for a door-to-door sales call, I thought. *Talking to this guy is just a procrastination strategy. I should tell him I don't have time.*

But before I could speak, Milano started in with his spiel about the company he worked for and how they were teaching him how to work and giving him a chance to earn scholarships for college. He said he came from the "hood" in Los Angeles and that this job had changed his life. He was traveling across the country selling magazines and wanted to show me the great selection he had. He said his name was Milano, "You know, like the cookie!" Milano was working his lines hard, but not so much talking to me, as talking at me, delivering a memorized sales monologue, a little too fast, but complete with perfectly placed exclamation points and question marks.

I had read about these enigmatic companies that send kids

around the country to sell magazines door-to-door. The article detailed how some of them take advantage of the kids, putting them up in cheap hotels, and barely paying them enough to eat and meet travel expenses. So my first question for Milano (before telling him I didn't have time for him) was not about magazines, but about whether he was actually being paid and treated fairly. My question took him a little by surprise and forced him off his sales script.

"Oh yeah!" he said. His boss was great, the company really wanted to help young people like him turn their lives around, learn responsibility, and get to college. He said this job was teaching him to set goals and be responsible and made him realize the value of hard work. Milano said that in L.A. he had been raised on food stamps and "general relief" and that he had never really learned to work. He said his mama was a "drinker and a smoker" but she pulled her life together and wanted him to do the same.

As he spoke my feelings for this stranger at my door were at once motherly, protective, and suspicious. I hoped it was true that the company was not taking advantage of him, and I admired his desire to make a new life for himself. I loved the idea that he found a program, a job, and people who could help him pull out the greatness that is inside of everyone to create a life of self-sufficiency, contribution, and pride. And certainly it struck me that this was the very thing I was supposed to be writing about up in my office where the screen was still blinking.

But on another less transcendent level of my thinking mind, I was still a bit dubious. I began adding to the cacophony of thoughts and worry in my brain by making the split-second judgments and assumptions that I tend to make with door-to-door solicitors and car dealers. Like, "Is this guy for real? Is his smile a mask? Is his "personal story" just a manipulation? Am I just another "target" at just another door?" I figured he was a bit dubious too, and, in another microsecond, I made more assumptions and arrogantly assigned them to him! I imagined he looked around our neighborhood and looked at me and thought "Middle-aged white lady in a nice house – what does she know about anything? What does she know about my life? She's not a real person."

But just as I surprised Milano with my question about the fairness of his job, he surprised me with questions about my life. He wanted to know about my parents, and my first job, and did I go to college. I told him about my jobs at "the Mall" as a teenager, and how I saved enough money in high school to pay for my entire first year of college on my own. As we talked we both relaxed. He dropped the "sales guy" routine and I dropped my internal dialogue about whether I had time to talk to him or what his preconceived notions about me and my ability to buy magazines might be.

He said he imagined I had a real nice mom and dad who taught me right from wrong and how to work. Of course, I said he was right about that. Then he said, "You did a lot on your own, but your mom and dad were always standing there behind you, weren't they." Maybe this was an obvious assumption for him to make. But there was something about the way he said it, and the look on his face, that seemed so prescient.

He said it like he knew us. Like he had been hovering above us when my parents talked about the importance of work and independence, and he understood how their caring teaching and guidance gave me the foundation to build my own life of self-sufficiency and contribution. He said it like he was there all those times when I was his age and I needed help to stay standing; the times when my mom and dad were there for me with meals, and paint brushes, and moving vans, and extra cash to make the rent. Milano's reminder of the good fortune of my birth to loving parents gave the first hint that the fog in my head might dissipate that afternoon.

Milano said he liked talking to people about their lives and that he thought he could learn a lot from people in the neighborhoods where he sold magazines. He told me that he talked to a guy the day before who taught him the word "innate." He said he liked the word and asked me to confirm the definition. I said, "Yeah, it's something, some quality, that is naturally inside of you." Then he said, "I can see that you are an innate self-starter. You get stuff done."

He hit another nerve. That summer my mind was so polluted with self-destructive worry and deep self-doubt, that an irrational belief that I was *not* accomplishing *anything* meaningful pervaded my perceptions. I was drowning in fears that I was not living up to my potential and constantly comparing myself to other working parents who were able to keep it all in balance – excellent professionalism, loving childrearing, creative pursuits, marital romance, deep friendships, and optimal physical fitness - in a way that was simply out of my limited grasp. Milano's straight-forward and unconditional statement of faith in me reminded me of my dad, whose definitive way of expressing his confidence in me always made me believe him. Sunlight began to penetrate the fog.

"What do you do now for work?" he asked me.

I confessed that I was procrastinating at that very moment, and that I should have been up at my desk instead of talking to him. I told him about the grant writing and my clients and the philanthropists and the deadline. I told him how it all stresses me out sometimes, but that I felt incredibly blessed to have so much good work and the ability to work from home where I am near my children.

Somewhere along the line of our unlikely conversation, I told him I would buy a couple of magazines – even though I really didn't need any more paper in my house, and I really didn't have time to read magazines. As he was filling out the order form, Milano said, "Let me ask you something. You're involved in philanthropy in your work every day. Why are you helping me?"

"Well," I said, "I'm working on a grant right now to help young people like you find a way into decent jobs and out of poverty. I spend a lot of time writing about the problems of these kids, and how they need support and adults to show them that they care and believe in them to succeed. Most of the time I'm just sitting alone in my little office upstairs writing 'about' these kids and their lives, instead of engaging 'with' them. But here you are. You are a real person who has come to my door asking me – a real person – to help you. How could I say no?"

It was true. Milano was not a hypothetical character in a grant proposal. He was not a statistic in a chart or table I was creating to demonstrate "Need." He was not a blinking abstraction on my computer screen. He was a human being, with a mama, and a history, and dreams, and the *chutzpah* to be riding around the country on a bus selling magazines to strangers.

With his clipboard, dog-eared forms, and pen in hand, Milano looked at me like he was going to cry. "Thank you," he said. "You know so many people say to me, 'I'm already doing this. I'm already doing that. I don't have time.' And they slam the door in my face because they say they're already doing their part. People can be cruel. But what you just said there – that was real."

A lump formed in my throat. The fog in my brain was gone. The cacophony of worry was silenced, and I could feel the full light and heat of the summer sun. Somehow Milano and I had created a clear space of presence and life and connection. A space that was real.

We finished up the paperwork, and I offered Milano a can of soda for the road. He said he stays away from soda, but asked if he could have some water. We don't buy bottled water, so I had to bring him a glass from the kitchen and we stood on the porch chatting some more. Milano said that he had been diagnosed with ADD (Attention Deficit Disorder) as a kid. He talked some more about his family, and about being raised on public assistance. He said he was a late bloomer and that before he had this job he never knew how to set a goal, let alone reach one.

Despite the obvious challenges of door-to-door sales, he said he was inspired by the people he met along the way who were good to him. He said he learned from them and learned that no one gets anything for nothing. "You have to work hard," he said. "Even people who look like they have everything have had to work for it most of the time."

His curiosity about people and his ability to find the good amid the slammed doors and personal rejection that are standard working conditions in a job like his were admirable. More than that, it felt again like this person on my doorstep had a deeper message for me. Like he wanted to remind me that whatever our work in this life - everyone has challenges and difficulties to face and overcome. There will be deadlines, difficult personalities, and minutia. Deal with it. Accept it. Keep your eyes focused on the goal, and look for the good amid the struggle. But don't give up. Whatever the job or goal or dream - keep moving forward.

Then in his uncommon and prescient way, he said, "I know

you're working on something - wanting something big."
Without telling Milano, I instantly thought about my dreams
of writing this book and spending my days untangling the
experience of life through art and stories.

Once more, with the 100% brand of confidence that my dad
always had in matters such as these, Milano said, "You're
going to get what you want. I'm sure of that."

"I *am* working on something," I admitted. "And it means so
much to me that you would say that. Thank you."

As if he were much older and much wiser and much more
confident than I, Milano looked straight into me, and rather
swiftly replied, "Don't thank *me*."

I was struck silent by this unusual response. As I took it in I
felt a wave of gratitude for my family, my neighborhood, my
work, the sun, the moon, the earth, and the incomprehensible
forces of the universe responsible for such things as
arranging a meeting between Milano and me.

Then he thanked me for the water and the magazine sale and
the chat. He shook his head and said, "You never know what
kind of impact you have on a person. You never know."

He said he hoped I enjoyed my magazines, but warned me that they don't arrive quickly. "Now don't git fidgety sista!" he said, in his most casual vernacular, as if we were regular old friends. "It takes 90 to 120 days for these subscriptions to start. You hear that? So don't git fidgety." It was a funny thing to say to one of his customers, and the exact kind of word choice, timing, and delivery that strikes my funny bone. He could tell.

We laughed and shook hands. Milano's grip was firm and serious and warm and he held my hand for a long minute. Then he opened the porch door, hopped off the steps, and skipped down the street. Literally.

As I watched him go, my heart felt huge and warm and alive. I skipped up to my office, journaled about my meeting with Milano, and finished my grant proposal with renewed purpose. I was reconnected, recharged, and filled with the certainty that Milano and me and everything in between are, in fact, the very breath of this whole big world of stories and possibilities and creeping flies and proposal deadlines and infinity.

Reflection Points

My encounter with Milano reminds me that none of us are really "strangers." We share so much common ground as human beings. When we stretch our minds just a little bit beyond the static cardboard caricatures of one another that we have built and sustained with stale thinking – we find true human connection.

◆ Can you remember a chance meeting or unlikely conversation with a stranger – even if you just exchanged a few words or glances? What were the circumstances of your meeting? What inspired you to engage with the stranger, rather than look away or close the door, as we so often do? What did you learn about that person or yourself because of the encounter? Jot down your memories in your **Mindful Gratitude Journal**.

◆ Have you ever had an unexpectedly meaningful conversation with someone you already knew? Have you ever opened up to a co-worker, neighbor, friend, or family member about something personal and made a deeper connection with that person – if only for a moment? Feel some gratitude for the spark of intuition that inspired you to open up in a new way, and write a few notes about the experience in your **Mindful Gratitude Journal**.

■ Take some time to remember the people who have contributed to your life by teaching or modeling the positive qualities, practices, skills, and values upon which you have built any success in your life – large or small. In your **Mindful Gratitude Journal**, make a list of these people and jot down what you have learned from them.

■ Are you a philanthropist? Most Americans and people around the world are! Most of us volunteer or make financial contributions to all kinds of non-profit and religious organizations. Who benefits by your gifts? You are connected to those individuals! Feel a wave of gratitude for your ability to give and to be connected to all those people!

■ Do you enjoy museums, the zoo, your local performing arts groups? Are there homeless shelters, youth programs, food pantries, schools, and other organizations that make your community a safer, healthier place to live? These organizations and resources are supported by philanthropists who make contributions large and small. In your **Mindful Gratitude Journal**, make a list of the organizations that are meaningful to you and send thoughts of gratitude to all the people whose financial investments bring those ideas, performances, and services to life!

The Only Life
We Know Of

"You could have been born a plant or a planet or a star or anything else. But you were born a person, and people are the only living things who can talk. It's really special to be a person."

My son Charlie, my nighttime philosopher, was contemplating life again from the heights of his loft bed.

As a fifth grader Charlie has not lost one ounce of the pure good energy that flowed from him the moment he was placed on my chest for the first time at St. Mary's Hospital and immediately began sucking on my chin as if to kiss me hello after being away for a very long time. He still likes it when I lay in bed with him at the end of the day to chat and hold hands. He is open and positive and life-loving.

"There are only like a billion people on earth," Charlie said.

More like 7 billion, I thought, but I certainly didn't want to interrupt.

"That's a tiny amount in the whole huge universe. We are on a tiny planet – a tiny part of one galaxy, and for all we know, we are the only people in the whole galaxy. So to be one of those people, to be born a human is REALLY important."

Charlie had been studying astronomy in his science class at school. All of that fascinating new information about the universe was feeding his core life philosophy - the philosophy that has led him to embrace his family and friends and snowboarding and biking and sailing and playing lacrosse with mad enthusiasm. A usually unarticulated but vividly lived philosophy that says life is a precious gift meant to be celebrated.

Recognizing that I was in for some beautiful bedtime musings, I grabbed a nearby pen and notebook, propped myself up on my elbows, and began taking down Charlie's words verbatim so that I would not forget them in my usual end-of-day haze. Charlie lay on his back next to me, relaxed, unselfconscious, and fully in flow.

"There are nine planets in our solar system," he continued, making his point with growing conviction, "and we live on the ONLY planet with people. To be living on one of those planets and to be one of those points of light in the galaxy is amazing. *We're the only life we know of.*"

This seemed a brilliant revelation to me. He was right. In the enormity of this and multiple other known galaxies, WE are the only intelligent life we know of. Even if there are nearly 7 billion of us, and even if there is intelligent life somewhere in a distant galaxy, we are proportionally rare beings in the infinite vastness of the cosmos.

Compared to the trillions of grains of sand shifting on the beaches, blades of grass growing from the ground, water molecules floating in the oceans, species of animals, birds, flowers, plants and endless other forms of life on earth, humans, with our distinct gifts of consciousness and language, are uncommon entities on our own planet, let alone the galaxy! More than that, Charlie went on to emphasize that each person is completely unique and of the utmost individual significance.

"People think movie stars are so great, but they are just people who have a lot of money and fame. They aren't better than anyone. Everyone is equally important. YOU are really special. Anyone who has lived, or will live, or is presently living is VERY LUCKY."

Then Charlie gently waved his hand in a circular motion around my face and said "This will never be on this earth again after you die. It's really important that we live this life wisely," he said, "because you only get to live it once."

Charlie's innocent wisdom felt simultaneously like a soft blanket and a stern dose of advice from an experienced elder. It was mid-December, and my mind was clogged with worries about work, family, and all those Christmas presents I still needed to buy. I was tired and feeling low that night. But here was Charlie, reminding me that this body, this brain, this life was now – and it would never be on this earth, under these circumstances, ever again after I die. So I better treat it all with care. I better recognize and enjoy the magnificence in all this NOW.

Charlie's observations jolted me outside of myself and my own little world of worries and personal priorities and reminded me that I am not alone. I am sharing this planet with 7 billion other souls – all of them worthy of my respect, if only for the sheer fact of their existence as rare beings in our infinite universe and for their essential role in the epic story of the human race.

Each life, no matter the circumstances, is a deep and beautiful mystery filled with unique meaning and inextricably linked to every other life on the planet. Conceived by the power of an invisible force and made to grow like the flowers and the trees, we are all miracles of nature - wonders of the world.

Your dentist. Your neighbor. The disagreeable checkout clerk at the grocery store. Your favorite movie star and YOU. From the slums of Mumbai to the green farms of Wisconsin. Across the globe and back again. Rich or poor, black, brown or white, male or female, religious or not, our individual value is immeasurable and our contributions to one another, seen and unseen, are infinite.

Yet, in the midst of our busy lives, it's easy to miss the meaning and magic hidden in our seemingly common experiences and everyday interactions with one another. Sometimes we feel weighted down by the responsibilities of work and family. Sometimes we are overburdened by illness, financial distress, difficulties in our relationships, and other struggles. Sometimes, we feel ordinary and small in world that seems vast and dominated by forces beyond our control.

Sometimes we truly believe we are alone.

But our depth, beauty, and unbreakable connection to all of humanity exist and persist whether we are aware of them or not. From the grand scientific discoveries that alter life for the better forever, to the small kindnesses exchanged in neighborhoods, schools, homes and workplaces all over the world, now, more than at any other time in human history, our lives are an ongoing gift to one another.

The imprints of humanity – of thousands of unseen human hands – literally permeate our lives. This is particularly true in the West, where our clothing, food, medicines, tools, furniture, soaps, toothpaste, gadgets, and appliances are rarely made by us. They appear in our lives deceivingly easily through mindless little shopping trips or a few clicks on the internet. But in reality these things are the products of countless hardworking individual engineers, designers, factory workers, farmers, distributors, managers, bankers, truck drivers, and store clerks.

Walk back almost anything you own and an intricate map of human contribution quickly emerges. At every step, from new idea to product on a store shelf, our favorite things are touched by the hands of individual people, each with his or her own story. People who got up for work on innumerable

unmarked mornings and despite their personal challenges -
feeling tired, sick kids, an argument at home – went to work
and did their bit to produce the items that we love and rely
upon.

Look at the clothing on your body. Look around wherever you
are. How many human hands did it take to create whatever
you are looking at? How much thought, creativity, planning,
decision-making, skill, talent and contribution did it take to
manifest each item within your sight?

When I really stop to absorb this concept - the realization that
I am NEVER alone – truly takes my breath away. My entire
reality is covered with the miraculously distinctive fingerprints
of millions of people whom I will never see, but whose daily
work is visible, audible, and tangible in my home, my office,
and throughout my whole community.

In every moment of every day, there is an endless chain of
individuals across the globe and all over my community,
working to meet my needs.

RIGHT NOW there is a farmer growing vegetables that my
family will someday eat.
RIGHT NOW there are people working in utilities companies
ensuring that heat, electricity, clean water, and phone service

are mine at the press of a button.

RIGHT NOW there are journalists in every corner of the globe taking photographs, interviewing people I could never meet, interpreting events, writing stories, and often risking their personal safety so that I can understand what's going on in the world.

RIGHT NOW there are writers and comedians skillfully hunched over their computers tapping out books, movies and the next episodes of my favorite shows, so that I can be informed, enlightened, and entertained.

RIGHT NOW there are musicians and artists putting their hearts on the line so that my life will be filled with the rich sounds and colors of their imaginations.

RIGHT NOW there are young people studying to become my future doctor, hair stylist, plumber, electrician, and president.

RIGHT NOW teachers everywhere are preparing children to read and write and think and create.

RIGHT NOW there are philanthropists making financial contributions to my local museums, libraries, parks, hospitals, schools, food pantries and homeless shelters to make my community a better place to live.

RIGHT NOW there are people waking up and going to work in factories across the globe to make hundreds of useful items that will eventually make their way into my life and make it more convenient, or beautiful, or livable.

RIGHT NOW there are parents around the world raising children with the values of honesty, fairness, justice, responsibility, and cooperation so that our world will survive.

How can it be that we so often overlook our HUGE contributions to one another? How is it that with so many people working literally around the clock for us that we can ever feel small or lacking or alone? The truth is that we are ever abundant, constantly in community, and of essential importance to the balance of all that is good. All of our contributions matter, and the results of our contributions can be found everywhere. How can we NOT be in a constant state of gratitude and awe and respect for the miracle of the human race?

How can we ever miss what Charlie so easily saw after a few basic fifth grade astronomy classes? That to be one of only 7 billion people on this small blue planet spinning through a galaxy of 400 billion stars in a universe populated by billions of OTHER galaxies – makes every single person we know, or see, or think about a rare and sacred gift. Someone who, through his or her work, or influence on others, or simple breathing existence is a vital artery connected to the beating heart of all of humanity.

This awareness of and sense of gratitude for, humanity's gifts can, at times, be difficult to cultivate and easy to resist. Our personal biases, experiences, and circumstances often cloud our perception of the goodness that surrounds us. In our fast-paced world, where we sometimes don't even know the names of our neighbors, we can feel isolated, lonely, and maybe even cynical. We may look at our food or our favorite chair and say, "Well those people who made this chair didn't do it for ME personally. They were just going to work to earn their wages."

Maybe so. But this does not negate the fact that they made the chair, and someone designed the chair, and humanity has created an astounding system for production and distribution of all kinds of goods and services that allowed the chair and all kinds of other good and useful things to appear in our lives. It certainly doesn't mean that we can't feel deep gratitude for the chair and the people who made it, no matter the other circumstances of our lives.

Michaelangelo did not paint the Sistine Chapel for the millions of visitors who have flown around the planet to visit it. He couldn't even have conceived of the ways that his work has been reproduced and seen by generations of people around the globe. Yet his lack of awareness of the extensive, centuries-long impact of his work, makes it no less a gift to every individual who is touched by its beauty. His lack of awareness, much like the lack of awareness of those on the assembly line who make our favorite items, is no reason not to feel a deep sense of personal gratitude for his contributions to the world and our own sense of awe and inspiration at seeing his work.

Cultivating Mindful Gratitude is about developing a keen awareness of the goodness that exists in the world and touches our lives, NO MATTER our immediate circumstances. Our easy access to the gifts of humanity, from a simple delicious vegetable grown by a local farmer or a favorite chair, to the world's greatest works of art, are what make the practice of Mindful Gratitude such an accessible gateway to a sense of joy and contentment and connection.

"We're pretty much like one gi-normo family," Charlie said near the end of his celestial reflections. "You might say your family members are the most important, or you might look up to your mom or dad. But really you have thousands of mothers and fathers and millions of brothers and sisters. Like one family, WE are all those billions of people. *You have a tiny part of everyone on this earth in you.*"

Of all of Charlie's musings that night (and there were quite a few more – about war and peace and behaving justly - that simply did not fit into this little essay!) I found this final statement to be the most profound.

"You have a tiny part of everyone on this earth in you."

There is something so intuitively true about this, yet so completely mysterious. It speaks to that spark of recognition that we sometimes catch in the eyes of "strangers." It speaks to the theory of evolution which maintains that we were all born stars and that our physical forms are, indeed, the refined and evolved residue of stardust that first burst into existence billions of years ago. More mystically, it speaks to the beautiful teachings of Buddha, Jesus, and the other great spiritual leaders that we are all one body, one spirit, one life.

That a ten-year old boy articulated this mystery with such clarity from the heights of his loft bed on a mid-December night early in the 21st Century should really be no more astounding than that he breathes. Charlie is for sure enormously gifted. Yet, he is also a most normal boy. He has to work hard at school. He sometimes argues with his big sister and little brother and gets angry at his parents. His gift is one bestowed upon all of us at birth – a curious, open, loving heart. Charlie just happens to have a knack for listening very closely to the truths living in his heart and for unselfconsciously sharing what he hears.

What Charlie heard that night, about the miracle of our existence and the precious nature of every person on earth, is the very essence of the practice of Mindful Gratitude. It is the reminder to listen more carefully to ourselves and each other, to look more closely at the details that surround us, to notice more curiously, share more openly, and appreciate entirely.

Mindful Gratitude is the deep awareness that all the work and creation and pain and laughter and tears and love of the whole wide world live inside of everyone, gently calling for our unwavering compassion, reverence, and gratitude for all 7 billion members of Earth's extraordinary family.

Reflection Points

There is so much human history and depth in just about any item we can see or touch or hear - each containing a piece of the story of the people who created it. Look at the clothing on your body. Look around the room you are in. Take a few minutes to recognize how humanity has conspired to meet your needs in this moment. Now use your **Mindful Gratitude Journal** to record your answers to some of these questions:

- What are you enjoying right now? A cup of coffee? Your favorite music? A chair or blanket that is especially cozy? The view of your neighbor's flower garden? Your car? Make a list of the things you LOVE in your life and take a moment to acknowledge the long chain of individuals whose work brought those things into being.

- What is your contribution to the world? What does your daily work bring to others? No matter what you are doing, there is no doubt someone or many people who are benefiting by your work. Push out your thinking and imagine ALL of the people who are touched by your work. What does it mean to them? Now bring your thinking closer to home and imagine what you bring to your co-workers, friends and family.

◆ Take a moment to close your eyes and listen to your heart? What profound or simple messages of truth do you hear? Write down any insights or impressions that come to you.

◆ Get out a **Mindful Gratitude Notecard** or whatever notecards or stationary you have handy and write some short notes to people who make your life better in small or large ways. These may be people who you love and know well and see everyday, such as family members, your child's teacher, your co-workers or neighbors. OR you may think of someone whose name you don't even know, such as the sanitation men who take away your garbage, your mail carrier, the person who takes your coffee order every morning. Imagine how you could make them feel by tucking a note into their hands and letting them know that you have noticed how their work makes a difference in the world!

Acknowledgements

It is both extremely easy and very difficult to acknowledge everyone who helped create this book. Easy because I can truly thank every person I have ever met for contributing to my life, my experiences, and the perspective that allowed me to write these essays. Difficult because plenty of specific individuals played important roles throughout this epic process.

The book started as an idea one afternoon when a friend delivered dinner shortly after our son George was born. My dad had recently been diagnosed with terminal cancer, and I was overwhelmed by my new status as mother-of-three. I was so grateful for that dinner that I cried. I also noticed what a gift it is to feel gratitude.

I noticed that my gratitude – for that delicious dinner, and for our helpful friends, and for my safe house, and for the farmers who grew the food that my friend delivered – was my salvation. It was gratitude that kept me from falling into a dark hole of worry and sadness.

That idea grew into a book thanks to the encouragement, patience, tolerance, and gifts of many friends, colleagues, and family members.

The first word of gratitude must go to my parents, Nancy Wendelberger and the late, great George Wendelberger, who taught me from my earliest memories to celebrate the good things in life and to always say thank you. The next word goes to Timothy Meyerring for his early encouragement, constant faith in this project, steadfast patience, gorgeous artwork, and for the words that pushed me farther than I thought I could: "You need to write more."

Many early "readers" provided important feedback and much-needed encouragement including Lisa Grosz, Colleen Fitzgerald, Rebecca de Vogel, Heidi Wick, Michael de Vogel, David de Vogel, Margaret Phillips, and Mary Rasmussen who each told me in his or her own beautiful way that what I was doing was worth continuing.

After a long dormant period, dear friends Pam Miller and Sarah Hammond gently tapped my shoulder and reminded me that everyone deserves wellness and peace. Without that tap, I might not be writing this today. Joy Peot-Shields and Jim Shields opened the doors to their beautiful homes and repeatedly offered refuge, delicious meals, and supportive friendship that allowed me to rest, recharge, and reinvest in this project. Wise editing and eagle-eye proofreading were provided by Kathy Giorgio, Rebecca de Vogel, and Kathleen Zimmer-Anderson.

Special thanks to James Kaszubowski for creating an inspirational early prototype and to Laurette Perlewitz and Michael Tischer for brilliant brainstorming, technical assistance, and planning support at a critical moment in time. Mary Phillips, thank you for being a steady, thoughtful, creative and most reliable design partner.

I am very grateful for the many people who heard about this project and always asked how it was going. A few of them just could not leave me alone about it. Thank you Mom and Dennis Schroeder for never letting me off the hook.

Finally, thank you to my loving family. Michael, you have a Golden Soul, and your love and friendship pulled me through. Lulu, Charlie, and George, you have taught me most of what I know about courage, unconditional love, and acceptance. You are gifts beyond anything I could have ever dreamed up.

For all of you, I am eternally grateful.

About the Author

Christel B. Wendelberger is a writer and communications consultant living in Milwaukee, Wisconsin. She is the founder of Forward Communications, a firm specializing in strategic communications, executive coaching, fund development, and writing services for non-profit organizations.

As a strategic thought and communications specialist, Christel has a guiding faith in the essential goodness and infinite potential of every individual to play a transformational role in his or her own inner life, family, community and the world. Her work reflects a deep belief that within every individual and organization there exists a treasure trove of ideas that when deeply explored and clearly articulated represent the seeds of human progress.

Christel also leads dynamic interactive seminars on grant writing, philanthropy, and mindfulness. *Mindful Gratitude: Practicing the Art of Appreciation* is now a unique workshop and retreat designed for workplaces, community centers, and other groups.

Christel is married to her best friend and is the mother of three miraculous children whose sheer existence is a source of endless gratitude.